lex:tra

Grundwortschatz

Englisch

nach Themen

Übungsbuch

Brigitte Nikolai

Cornelsen

Grundwortschatz
Englisch nach Themen – Übungsbuch
von Brigitte Nikolai

Redaktion: Maria Funk
Umschlaggestaltung: Cornelsen Verlag Design
Umschlagfoto: JUNOPHOTO
Layout und technische Umsetzung: Buch und Gestaltung, Britta Dieterle
Illustrationen: Detlev Schüler

Weitere Titel in dieser Reihe
ISBN 978-3-589-01561-0 Grund- und Aufbauwortschatz Englisch nach Themen
ISBN 978-3-589-22447-0 Lerngrammatik Englisch

www.lextra.de
www.cornelsen.de

1. Auflage, 1. Druck 2008

Alle Drucke dieser Auflage sind inhaltlich unverändert und können im Unterricht nebeneinander verwendet werden.

Druck: CS-Druck CornelsenStürtz, Berlin

ISBN 978-3-589-01562-7

Inhalt gedruckt auf säurefreiem Papier aus nachhaltiger Forstwirtschaft.

Vorwort

Das Übungsbuch **Grundwortschatz Englisch nach Themen** hilft Ihnen beim Lernen des englischen Grundwortschatzes. Es präsentiert und übt die häufigsten 2000 Wörter des Englischen, die im Lernwörterbuch **Grund- und Aufbauwortschatz Englisch nach Themen** enthalten sind. Der Lextra Grund- und Aufbauwortschatz nach Themen ist eine neue Generation von Grund- und Aufbauwortschätzen, die das lexikalische Minimum, das notwendig ist für erfolgreiches produktives wie rezeptives Sprachhandeln, aufgrund empirischer Studien erfassen. Der Grundwortschatz Englisch basiert auf einer aktuellen Auszählung des englischen Wortschatzes (Leech, Rayson & Wilson 2003).

Das Übungsbuch **Grundwortschatz Englisch nach Themen** fasst den Grundwortschatz des Englischen in 76 übersichtlichen, nach Kategorien geordneten Kapiteln zusammen. Jedes Kapitel präsentiert und übt ca. 25 neue Wörter. Auf der linken Seite eines Kapitels werden die neuen Wörter vorgestellt und auf der rechten Seite werden Übungen dazu angeboten. Neue Wörter werden visuell und in Satzzusammenhängen in drei bis vier inhaltlich zusammengehörigen Abschnitten präsentiert. Viele Zeichnungen klären die Bedeutungen der neuen Wörter. Wörter, die nicht visuell eingeführt werden können, werden in einfachen Sätzen (Dialoge, kurze Erzählungen, Definitionen und Erklärungen) eingeführt. Die Sätze enthalten nur die Wörter des Grundwortschatzes.

Jedes Kapitel enthält ca. vier bis sechs Übungen, von leichten Zuordnungs- und Kategorisierungsaufgaben über etwas anspruchsvollere Lückentexte und andere satzbasierte Übungsformen zu produktiven Schreib- und Sprechaufgaben. Alle Aufgaben werden über eine inhaltlich orientierte Kurzüberschrift kontextualisiert, um bedeutungsorientiertes, inhaltliches Lernen zu garantieren. Die Aufgabe selbst wird durch eine einfache standardisierte Aufforderung gestellt.

Die Aufgaben haben das Ziel, die Bedeutung von Wörtern sowohl selbstständig als auch in Satzzusammenhängen einzuprägen. Die jeweils letzte Aufgabe eines Kapitels bettet die neuen Wörter in Ihre Lebenswelt ein und bittet Sie, auf persönliche Fragen mit diesen Wörtern zu antworten, um sie relevanter und einprägsamer für Sie zu machen. Diese Antworten sollten abwechselnd schriftlich und mündlich formuliert werden. Das mündliche Formulieren hilft als Vorbereitung für echte kommunikative Situationen, indem Sprechroutinen automatisiert werden. Das schriftliche Formulieren fördert die Genauigkeit und eine größere Ausdrucksfähigkeit.

Die besten Lernresultate erzielen Sie auf folgende Weise:

- Lesen Sie den Grundwortschatz des Kapitels in dem entsprechenden Kapitel des **Grund- und Aufbauwortschatzes Englisch nach Themen** und überprüfen Sie ein erstes Lernen daran, dass Sie die Übersetzung und den Beispielsatz dort abdecken und versuchen, sich an die Bedeutung des Wortes zu erinnern.
- Arbeiten Sie sich dann durch den Präsentationsteil des Übungsbuches und versuchen Sie, alle Sätze zu verstehen. Schlagen Sie unbekannte Wörter im Grund- und Aufbauwortschatz nach.
- Machen Sie dann die Übungen im Aufgabenteil. Schlagen Sie auch hier Wörter, an die Sie sich nicht erinnern können, nach.
- Wiederholen Sie Ihre Vokabeln in regelmäßigen Abständen. Wenn Sie zum Beispiel zehn Kapitel durchgearbeitet haben, lesen Sie noch einmal die Präsentationsseiten dieser zehn Kapitel, markieren Sie alle Wörter, an die Sie sich nicht mehr erinnern und schreiben Sie diese Wörter mit Übersetzungen und Beispielsätzen in ein Vokabelheft. Beantworten Sie die Fragen der letzten Aufgabe auf der rechten Seite des Kapitels.
- Beschäftigen Sie sich zusätzlich mit Ihrer Fremdsprache, indem Sie leichte Texte lesen, leichte Hörtexte hören und Gelegenheiten wahrnehmen, mit Muttersprachlern Ihrer Zielsprache auf einfache Weise zu kommunizieren.

Bedanken möchte ich mich bei Casey Hayes, Silke Lipinski, Anne Gadow, Timothy Price, Michelle Glauser und Erwin Tschirner, die bei der Erstellung der Kapitel geholfen haben, sowie bei Helga Holtkamp und Gunther Weimann vom Cornelsen-Verlag, die dieses Projekt geleitet und tatkräftig unterstützt haben, bei Maria Funk, unserer hervorragend organisierten und gewissenhaften Redakteurin und Projektmanagerin, sowie bei den vielen Mitarbeitern des Cornelsen-Verlags, die aus diesem Projekt ein so schönes Buch gemacht haben.

Ich wünsche Ihnen Spaß beim Lernen und hoffe, dass Ihnen das Übungsbuch **Grundwortschatz Englisch nach Themen** hilft, Ihre Sprachlernziele zu erreichen.

Brigitte Nikolai, Bad Harzburg im Sommer 2008

Inhalt

People

- Debbie Smith is a *woman*. You can call her "Mrs. Smith" or "Ms. Smith".
- Sometimes a *woman* is also called a *female*.

- Peter Norton is a *man*. You can call him "Mr. Norton".
- Sometimes a *man* is also called a *male*.

- Peter Norton and Debbie Smith are *persons* or *individuals*.

- James is a *boy* and Laura is a *girl*. James and Laura are *kids*.

- Mr. Norton and Mrs. Smith are *adults* because they are over 18 years old.
- *Seniors* are older people who have retired from working.
- *Youth* is the time of life between being a *kid* and being an *adult*. A *boy* of 15 is called a *youth*.

Identity

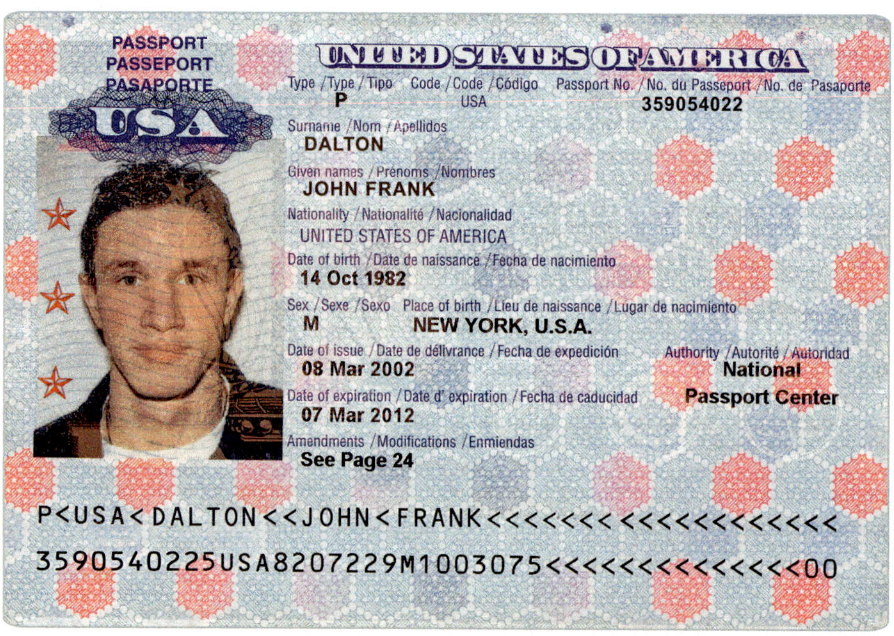

- John Dalton has a passport. He can be *identified* with this document.
- John was *born* in 1982. His date of birth is October 14. In the year 2008 his *age* was 26.
- John's middle *name* is Frank. He was *named* after his grandfather.
- John has brown hair and blue eyes and he is rather tall.

A Right or Wrong? Tick the right box.

		Right	Wrong
1	Mr Dalton is a man or a male.	☐	☐
2	You call all women "Ms.".	☐	☐
3	The sex of girls is female.	☐	☐
4	When you are 16 years old you are a youth.	☐	☐

B Age. Put the following words in order from youngest to oldest.

youth ▪ senior ▪ kid ▪ adult

____

C Identity. Complete the sentences using the following words.

born ▪ person ▪ name ▪ name ▪ identify ▪ sex ▪ age

1 We will ______________ the baby "Susan" after her grandmother.

2 He wrote "twenty-one" on the paper next to "______________".

3 His ______________ was John Jones.

4 Police tried to ______________ the man, but they could find no papers with a name on them.

5 Each ______________ was asked to fill out some papers while waiting.

6 Jane did not know if Lisa had a girl or a boy, so she asked, "What is the ______________ of the baby?"

7 The baby was ______________ at eight o'clock this morning.

D Now over to You … Answer the questions using the words from page six.

1 Draw an identification card (ID) for yourself using page six as a model.
2 Talk about yourself. Use the information on your ID.

Nationalities and Stereotypes

- *Europeans* can travel throughout the European Union without a passport.
- It is considered to be very *British* to have a cup of tea at five o'clock.
- The *English* language is spoken in many countries.
- The *French* produce the best wine in the world.
- *German* beer is exported all over the world.
- It is a *Scottish* tradition to drink whiskey.
- Limerick is an *Irish* town.

Europe and Beyond

- Tolstoy was a very famous *Russian* writer.
- In *Japanese* food, fish is very important.
- Many *American* movies are shown on *German* TV.
- In a *foreign* country, one has to get used to a different way of life.

Family

- Anne is Kevin's *mother*.
- Paul is Kevin's *father*.
- Anne and Paul are Sarah's *parents*. Sarah calls them *"Mum"* and *"Dad"*.
- Sarah is Anne's *daughter*.
- Kevin is Paul's *son*.
- Jane is a happy *child*. She was *adopted* when she was a *baby*.
- Sarah, Jane and Kevin are Paul's *children*.
- Paul is Anne's *husband* and Anne is Paul's *wife*.
- Anne and Paul belong to the same *generation*.
- Sarah and Kevin are *related*. They are *brother* and *sister*.
- Kevin loves his *dad*. They have a good *relationship*.

A The Family Tree on Page Eight. Complete the sentences using the following words.

adopted ▪ brother ▪ daughter ▪ husband ▪ mother ▪ parents ▪ sister ▪ son

1 Anne is the ______________ of three children.

2 Her ______________ Paul is from Scotland.

3 Paul enjoys playing soccer with his ______________ Kevin.

4 Anne loves to go shopping with her teenage ______________ Sarah.

5 Kevin and Sarah are ______________ and ______________.

6 Jane was ______________ when she was a baby.

7 Anne and Paul are Kevin's ______________.

B Family Terms: Part I. Match the words with their definitions or descriptions.

1 A wife
2 A baby
3 A family
4 Adopt
5 A parent

a is a group of people related to each other.
b is a new born child.
c is to accept someone to be a legal part of the family.
d is either the father or the mother of a person.
e is the woman a man is married to.

C Family Terms: Part II. Unscramble the groups of letters to fill in the blanks in the sentences.

1 The girl's ______________ PLTIANSHREOI to her mother is good because they spend a lot of time together.

2 Mary is five years old. She is a young ______________ LDHIC.

3 The first ______________ TREGENAION of the family only has two living members.

4 Susie loves both her parents, her ______________ MMU and her dad.

5 Bob was very happy when he heard about the ______________ TRHBI of his baby brother.

6 Her favourite parent to read a story to her at bedtime is her ______________ ADD.

D Odd One Out. Circle the word in each group that does not belong.

1 British – English – Japanese – foreign
2 English – French – Scottish – Irish
3 Europe – American – German – Russian

E Now over to You … Answer the questions using the words from page eight.

1 Do you have any brothers or sisters? How is your relationship with them?
2 What are your parents' names? How old are they? What is your family's nationality?
3 Do you know any people with a nationality other than your own? What is their nationality?
4 What is your native language? Do you study any other languages but English? Which ones? Which other languages are you interested in?

Age and Size

old

young

short

tall

thin

huge

small

tiny

The Way Things Look

- When a person smiles, he or she *appears* to be happy.
- Julia is only interested in her *image*. What other people think of her is very important.
- "Pretty" is another word for *beautiful*.
- A person with white skin is sometimes called *fair*.
- The police could identify the criminal because he had a *mark* on his face.
- The way you look is your *appearance*.
- Somebody who looks *beautiful* or interesting is *attractive*.
- Beautiful flowers *attract* lots of butterflies.
- Someone who has a lot of friends is *popular*.
- Someone, like Johnny Depp, who is known by a lot of people is *famous*.

Character

- For many people, *character* is more important than a *beautiful* face.
- The way you act toward people is your *behaviour*.
- Although Mark lost his job and his wife left him, he still has a positive *attitude* towards the future.
- Because Susan was always *nice* to her customers, she got a present.
- *Bright* is another word for intelligent.
- Lisa was sure that she would get the new job. Her new boss liked her *confidence* during the job interview.

Capability

- A person with a strong opinion is also called *firm*. Even though everyone else thought differently, Mary was *firm* in her belief.
- Annie claims she has the *ability* to look into the future, but nobody believes her.
- Poor John forgot his money. He is not *able* to pay for his beer.
- George is very strong. He is *capable* of lifting very heavy boxes.
- If you are not able to do something, you are *unable*. Jane tried, but she was *unable* to finish her homework before class.
- Something you have learned to do is a *skill*. Michael has lots of *skills*. He will soon find a new job.
- Although Jenny's life is hard, she has the *will* to keep going.

A Matching. Label the pictures with the following words.

beautiful ▪ bright ▪ small ▪ huge ▪ famous ▪ tiny

1 ______________________

2 ______________________

3 ______________________

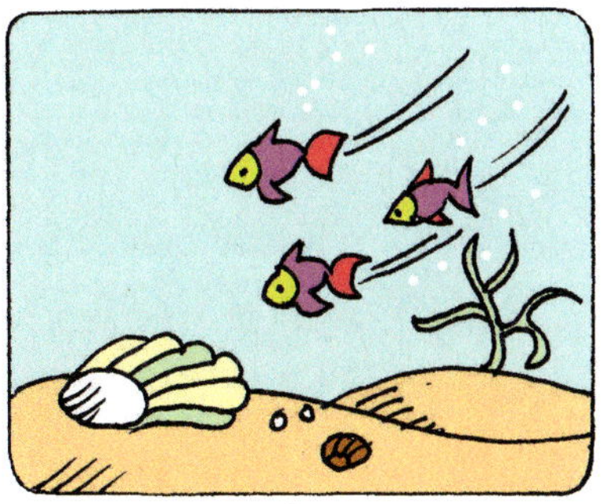

4 ______________________

5 ______________________

6 ______________________

B Synonyms. Replace the underlined words with the following words.

appears ▪ attracted ▪ fair ▪ firm ▪ skills ▪ unable

1 Lisa has very blond hair and white skin.
2 John always has strong opinions.
3 People are drawn to Tom because of his friendly character.
4 Chris was not able to finish his exam on time.
5 The mail box seems to be full.
6 Mary got the job because she has the knowledge to do it.

C Odd One Out. Circle the word in each group that does not belong.

1 old – huge – tiny – short
2 unable – capable – confidence – ability
3 nice – attractive – beautiful – appearance
4 character – behaviour – tall – will

D Now over to You… Answer the questions using the words from page ten.

1 Who is the most interesting person in your family? Describe their appearance and character.
2 Do you look up to someone famous? Explain what you like about this person.

Religion

- On Sunday, many *Christians* go to *church*.
- Different *religions* have different *beliefs*. *Christians believe in God* and the *Holy Spirit*.
- *Faith* is one of the most important aspects of *religion*.
- Unfortunately, the concept of *Hell* can also be found in different *religions*.
- *Mass* is a central part of Catholic *religion*.

Philosophy

- Gandhi fought for the *freedom* of India.
- Sometimes it seems easier to lie than to tell the *truth*.
- George is a policeman. It is his *duty* to protect people from dangerous criminals.
- You need a lot of *commitment* to work with handicapped children.
- Mohammed's *existence* can be proved from old texts.

Moral Duties and Beliefs

- Because of his strong *moral* values, Tim became a very *religious* person.
- Parents are *responsible* for their children. When Michael's mother and father go out they leave him with a babysitter.
- The Bible says, "You *shall* not kill, steal or speak badly about your neighbour."
- John believes that all *existing* things can either be seen, smelled or touched.
- Paul had an argument with his mother. He *ought* to apologise to her. He also *ought* to explain the reason for his behaviour.
- He said he was busy, but I do not think this is *true*.
- Everybody should *help* people who are in need. It is a *moral duty* to *help* poor people.
- Tom believes that things *exist* beyond the visible world and that there is life on other planets.

A Religion and Belief. Find nine words from this chapter in the word search.

C	R	R	A	S	Z	I	Z	S	E	X
U	U	M	V	A	T	R	U	T	H	L
B	O	R	A	B	V	B	C	C	N	C
M	A	F	O	S	I	R	I	O	E	H
C	H	A	Y	O	S	E	E	E	G	U
A	L	I	I	S	S	L	G	G	I	R
F	A	T	B	E	L	I	E	F	L	C
T	E	H	H	A	K	G	E	U	E	H
D	U	T	Y	S	P	I	R	I	T	F
T	R	A	N	Q	U	O	L	O	N	E
S	H	A	L	L	W	N	K	H	I	G

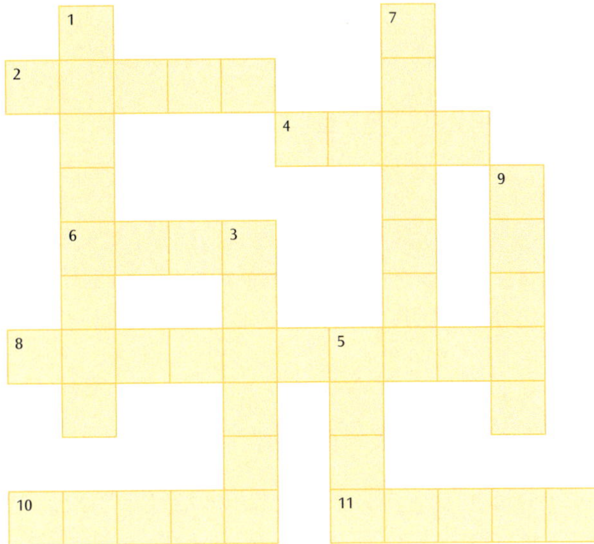

B Crossword Puzzle. Complete the crossword puzzle above with the following words.

believe ▪ commitment ▪ exist ▪ gods ▪ help ▪ Jesus ▪ Mass ▪ religion ▪ shall ▪ spirit ▪ truth

Down:
1 A particular way of worshipping is a …
3 A ghost is a type of …
5 One element of Christian celebration is …
7 To be sure that something is true is to …
9 Another word for 'fact' is …

Across:
2 People who believe in … are Christians.
4 To offer assistance is to … someone.
6 The Romans believed in many …
8 To work intensely means to show …
10 To be there is to …
11 Another word for 'should' is …

C Faith and Belief. Complete the sentences using the following words.

believe ▪ existence ▪ existing ▪ faith ▪ responsible ▪ truth

1 After his father died in a terrible car accident, Jim almost lost his ______________ in God.
2 Linda always takes on responsibility. She feels ______________ for all members of her family.
3 Peter is a very honest person. He always tells the ______________.
4 Tom believes in the ______________ rules of moral behaviour.
5 I cannot prove that there is a life after death, but I ______________ in it anyway.
6 We cannot deny the ______________ of poverty.

D Now over to You… Answer the questions using the words from page twelve.

1 What do you like about religion? What do you not like?
2 What moral concepts are important to you and/or your family?
3 What moral values are important in your culture?

House and Garden

Homes and Living

- *Estates* are large pieces of land with many nice *houses*.
- The *kitchen* is the room where people prepare food.
- Many people live in *flats*, especially when they cannot afford to buy a *house*.

- An *address* is what is written on letters to show where it should be delivered.
- A *block* is a section of a city divided from other sections by streets.

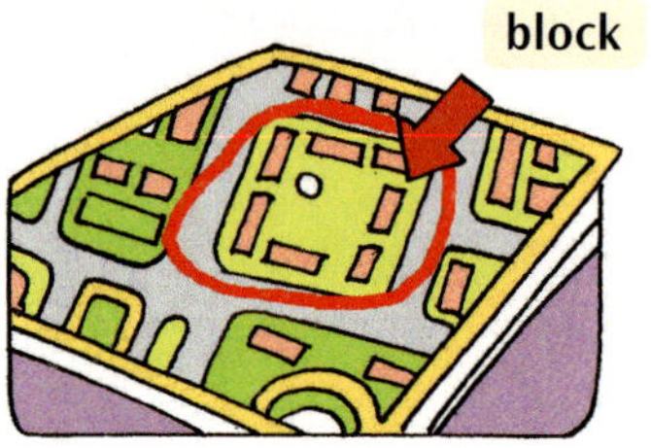

- Most *castles* were built by rich people who owned land.

Places to Live

- We often invite good friends to our *home*, but our *flat* was not big enough for all our friends.
- We lived in a huge *building* with twenty floors.
- We decided to *build* a new *house*.
- The new *house* was under *construction* for almost a year – quite a long time.
- It was built on a nice *estate* in the country, together with other new *homes*.
- Until our *house* was finished, we were *housed* in another *building*.
- A neighbour *lets* two rooms for students because his *house* is so big.
- Many couples share the *domestic* responsibilities, like cleaning, washing and shopping.

A Odd One Out. Circle the word in each group that does not belong.

1 floor – house – castle – building
2 window – house – wall – door
3 station – garden – kitchen – to let
4 block – station – domestic – estate

B Homes and Living. Complete the sentences using the following words.

castle ▪ block ▪ address ▪ castle ▪ garden ▪ flat ▪ kitchen ▪ estate ▪ station

1 She wrote her ______________ so he would know where her house was.
2 The new house is not in the city but on a nice ______________ in the country.
3 There was no park close to his house in the city, so he took his dog for a walk around the ______________.
4 The king and queen of that country lived in an old ______________ that had thick walls.
5 He lived in an inexpensive ______________ with four other people while he was a student in the city.
6 She was in the ______________ making dinner.
7 The train left the ______________ early in the morning.
8 The king lives in a beautiful ______________.
9 The house had a big ______________ with lots of flowers and trees.

C Puzzle. How many words from page 14 can you find in the puzzle?

T	B	P	M	H	Q	S	G
Q	G	H	V	V	P	T	A
R	Z	H	X	H	F	E	T
O	S	O	Z	O	G	P	E
O	N	M	B	U	I	L	D
M	C	E	Z	S	R	A	O
C	C	U	H	E	B	H	J
H	Y	Z	K	W	A	L	L

D Now over to You … Answer the questions using the words from page 14.

1 Do you live in a house or a building with flats? Describe your house or flat.
2 What is near your home? Are there any public buildings, parks or shops?
3 Do you have neighbours? Describe one of your neighbours and where they live.

Bedroom

Packing Up

Tom's family is packing up and moving out.

Moving Out

- Tom is moving into a new house. He has to move his whole *household* out of his old house.
- The kids have a lot of toys, clothes, and other things. Tom has to pack all of this *stuff* into boxes before the family can move into their new place.
- The kids' toys are in a large *cabinet*. The door on the *cabinet* is broken, so it won't close and the stuff inside keeps falling out.
- Before he moves the *cabinet* to the new house, Tom wants to *fix* the broken door.
- Tom tells his kids to go play outside in the *yard* while he fixes the *cabinet*.
- The kids run down the narrow *hall* between the rooms to go play outside. In the *hall* there are pictures of Tom's kids hanging on the wall.
- In the *entry*, the kids put on their shoes before opening the door to go outside.
- Tom needs a rest after his hard work, so he takes a *seat* in a chair outside and watches the kids playing in the *yard*.
- Tom sees more stuff to fix in the yard: a *board* has fallen off the wooden gate.
- He wants to go inside to get some tools, but the entry door is locked. Tom unlocks the door with a *key*.
- The kids are dirty from playing in the *yard*. Tom tells them to wash their hands with soap and water.

A Around the House. Match the following words with the pictures.

bed ▪ board ▪ cabinet ▪ key ▪ package ▪ table ▪ tape ▪ yard

1 ______________________

2 ______________________

3 ______________________

B Having a Visitor. Complete the sentences using the following words.

cover ▪ desk ▪ entry ▪ hall ▪ household ▪ objects ▪ seat ▪ sheet ▪ stuff

Paul, when you come to visit me at my new apartment, just ring the bell at the ____________[1]. Once you're in the building, walk down the long ____________[2]. I just moved out of my parents' house, so I don't have a lot of my own ____________[3]. I don't even have a ____________[4] to put on my bed! But I do stay warm in bed because I have a ____________[5]. And I do have a few empty boxes. You can use one as a ____________[6] to sit on. When I'm writing, I use another box as a ____________[7]. It's not much of a place to live yet, but at least now I am in my own ____________[8]. Dave, the student who lived here before, left some funny ____________[9] behind when he moved out.

C Household Stuff. Find the following words in the word search.

bedroom ▪ desk ▪ hall ▪ object ▪ package ▪ seat ▪ sheet ▪ tape

E	S	E	T	D	O	S	H	E	E	S	K	E	C	T	E	D
O	H	A	L	H	P	C	F	I	L	B	H	P	O	B	J	E
O	A	O	L	O	E	J	B	O	H	T	N	S	B	P	A	E
M	I	K	U	U	E	B	R	P	A	C	K	A	G	E	T	C
H	L	D	E	S	H	E	E	T	L	G	O	V	E	A	P	H
E	L	L	B	E	E	T	H	A	L	H	P	B	C	K	C	E
D	T	L	A	H	A	H	S	P	R	K	E	M	J	A	G	A
J	S	B	U	E	R	P	O	E	D	B	E	T	P	E	E	P
L	D	E	S	H	U	O	M	L	H	Y	H	F	A	G	C	F
B	E	D	R	O	O	M	L	I	D	E	S	K	J	Y	U	T

D Now over to You … Answer the questions using the words from page 16.

1 What does your bedroom look like? Draw a picture and label the items.
2 What things do you have on your desk/table at home?
3 Describe what you have in your cabinet. Is it tidy or untidy?
4 Have you ever moved into a new place? Describe what you need to do with all your stuff when you move.

World Map, Europe and the United Kingdom

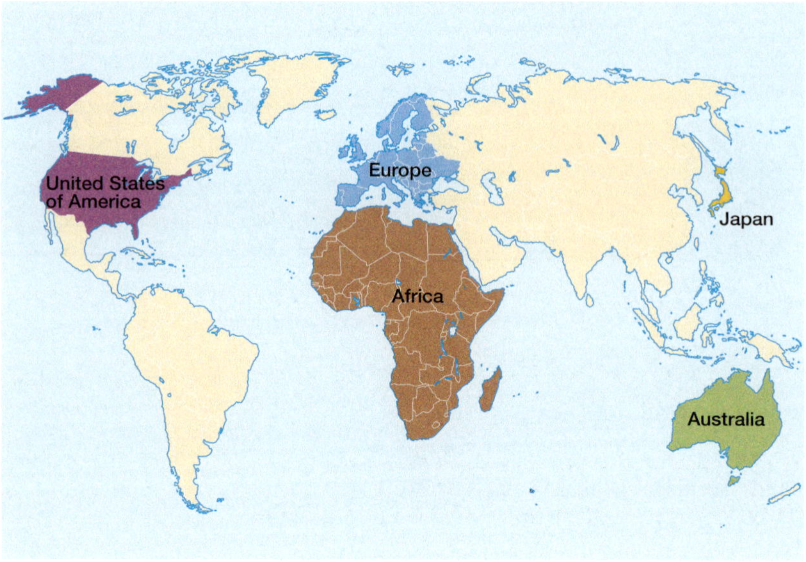

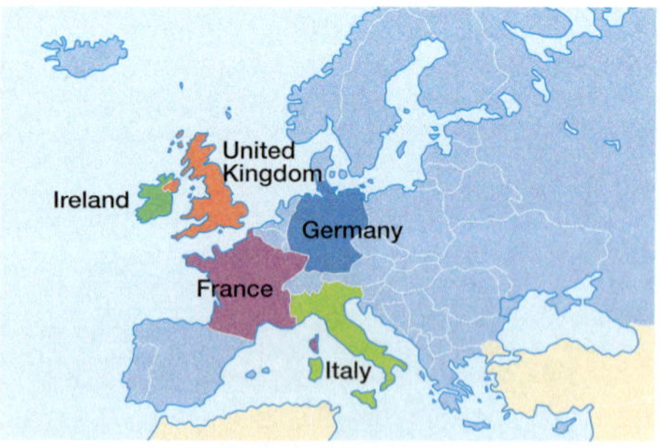

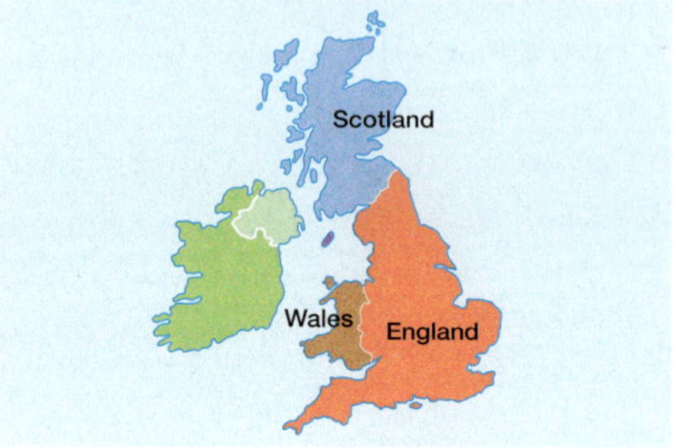

- On a map, the water is usually blue and the *land* is brown, yellow or green.
- *Germany* and *France* are *countries* in *Europe*.
- *Wales* and *Scotland* are *regions* of *Britain*.

Geography

- There is a *border* between *France* and *Germany*, but you do not have to show your passport. Both *countries* belong to the European Union.
-  The *bridge* across the river is old. It is not wide enough for cars.

- *Great Britain* is a big *island*, but *Australia* is bigger.
- The *capital* of *Britain* is London, the *capital* of *France* is Paris.
- A *city* is a very big place, a *town* is smaller and a *village* is usually very small.

Regions and Counties

- The South-West is a *region* of *Britain*. One of the best-known attractions there is Land's End. Other *regions* are the North and the Midlands.
- Each *region* in *Britain* has *regional* characteristics. The North, for example, has the Lake *District*.
- The Lake *District* in the northwest of *Britain* is famous for its national *park*.
- The national *parks* in the North and in Yorkshire offer a lot of natural beauty.
- Cornwall and Devon are *counties* in the South-East. *Britain* has many *counties*. Another well-known *county* is Kent, which is in the south with the *town* of Canterbury.

A Geography. Using page 18 and a map of Britain find examples for the following categories.

country	county	city	town	village

B Europe and the United Kingdom. Complete the sentences using the following words.

border ▪ capital ▪ countries ▪ counties ▪ district ▪ islands ▪ park ▪ regions

1 The West Midlands and the North East are ________________ of Britain.
2 The Lake ________________ is a famous tourist attraction in the north of the UK.
3 Italy and Ireland are ________________ in Europe.
4 A well-known national ________________ in Germany is in the northern part of the country.
5 Devon and Essex are ________________ in Great Britain.
6 Britain and Ireland are big ________________ in the North Sea.
7 Paris is the ________________ of France.
8 There is no ________________ between England and Wales because both are part of the UK.

C The World. Label the countries and continents.

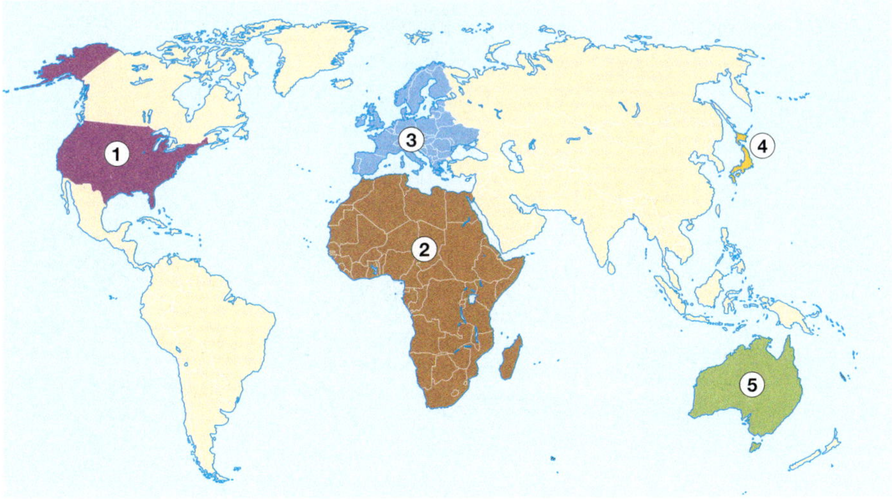

1 ________________
2 ________________
3 ________________
4 ________________
5 ________________

D Now over to You … Answer the questions using the words from page 18.

1 Where are you from? Do you live in a town or a village? What do you prefer, living in a town or city or in a rural area? Why?
2 Which big cities have you visited? What did you like and not like about them?
3 Have you been to other countries? What did you do there? Which attractions did you see?
4 Which countries would you like to visit and why? What would you like to do there?

Blue Planet

Landscape Types

Linda lives in the city. She enjoys the *urban environment*.
There are lots of fields and hills where Mike lives.
He lives in a *rural* setting.

The farmer grows his corn in his *field*.
In a *forest*, trees grow on their own.

Bodies of Water

Weather Report

Camp in the Mountains

- Susie likes to camp in the *mountains*. She enjoys a *natural environment*.
- She likes to get out of the city and into nature where she can enjoy the fresh *air*.
- Susie likes camping most when it is sunny and warm outside; that is when the *weather* is nice and the *sky* is blue.
- The *rivers* and *lakes* in the *mountains* are cold. Susie likes to swim in the clean *mountain water*.
- Sometimes she picks up *stones* or small *rocks* and throws them into the *lake*.
- Air, water, wind, and light are *natural resources*. Wood is another *natural resource*.

A Definitions. Match the words with their definitions or descriptions.

1 water
2 atmosphere
3 urban
4 rain
5 stone
6 temperature
7 world
8 forest
9 resource

a opposite of rural
b a small rock
c 24°
d natural gas, metal, wood
e an area with lots of trees
f the planet Earth
g water that falls from the sky
h chemical symbol: H_2O
i the air, clouds, and sky around Earth

B What Belongs Together? Organise the following words into three categories based on their common meaning.

lake ▪ rock ▪ pool ▪ air ▪ sky ▪ stone ▪ sea ▪ atmosphere ▪ mountain

C Crossword. Complete the crossword puzzle using the clues provided.

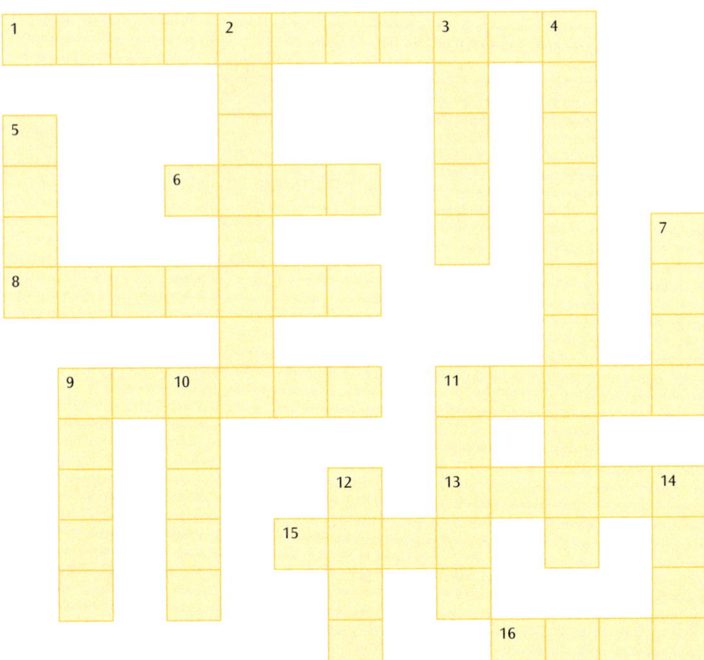

Across:
1 The natural world around us
6 A place where somthing is missing
8 Not man-made
9 A collection of trees
11 Cool drink
13 Outside of the city
15 High ground smaller than a mountain
16 Hills and valleys of water

Down:
2 Iron, oil, salt
3 The name of our planet
4 Very hot day, the … is 31°
5 A shower from the clouds
7 A small, bright light in the sky
9 Where corn is grown
10 A long, wide flow of water
11 Earth and all its people
12 Air that is moving fast
14 A large body of water amongst land

D Now over to You … Answer the questions using the words from page 20.

1 Do you like the rain? What is your favourite type of weather?
2 Do you live in a city or in the country? Describe the landscape around where you live.
3 Have you ever been camping? Describe what kinds of things you see when you camp.

The Course of a River

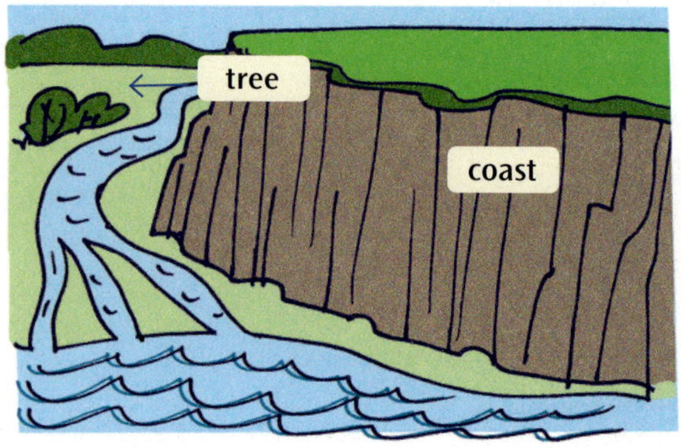

- A *valley* separates the *mountains*. There is a *river* flowing through the *valley*.
- The *valley* walls form the *banks* of the *river*. The *banks* of the *river* keep it on course.
- The *coast* is the area that separates the sea from the land. There is a beach on the *coast*.
- There is a *tree* growing next to the *river*. The *river water* helps the *tree* to grow.

A Tree Has Many Roles

Wild Animals

- The *water* from a *river* makes everything *grow* green and healthy. *Trees growing* closest to the *river* are the tallest and thickest.
- As a *tree grows* it gets thicker. One way to see the *growth* of a *tree* is to count the rings in its wood. The hard material from *trees* is used by humans to build houses and other buildings. *Wood* is a natural resource that *grows* in the wild.
- The *plants* on the *river banks* provide food for the *animals*. The *horses* are *animals* that eat the plants and drink the *river water*.
- There are many different types of *cats*. Some *species* of *cat* are not used to being around humans.
- A *horse* is a large animal. Humans ride on *horses*. *Cats* are small *animals*. They like to eat *fish*.
- *Horses* that do not live around humans are *wild*. Wild *animals* live in *nature*.
- There are many things that live in *nature* without the help of humans.

The Nature of Things

A True or False? Determine whether each sentence is true or false. For false sentences, provide a correct alternative.

		T	F
1	A group of similar animals or plants is a species.	☐	☐
2	Animals that live at your house are considered wild.	☐	☐
3	A fish is a type of fruit.	☐	☐
4	A river flows between its banks.	☐	☐
5	A valley is a small kind of river.	☐	☐

B Odd One Out. Circle the word in each group that does not belong.

1 egg – bird – valley – wing
2 plant – leaf – flower – growth
3 coast – tree – wood – branch

C Creatures. Label the pictures with the following words.

animals ▪ bird ▪ cat ▪ dog ▪ fish ▪ horse ▪ human

1 ____________

2 ____________

3 ____________

4 ____________

5 ____________

6 ____________

7 ____________

D Now over to You … Answer the questions using the words from page 22.

1 Do you have an animal? What is it? Describe your animal friend.
2 Do you like to grow things? Describe the types of plants that grow around your home.

Directions

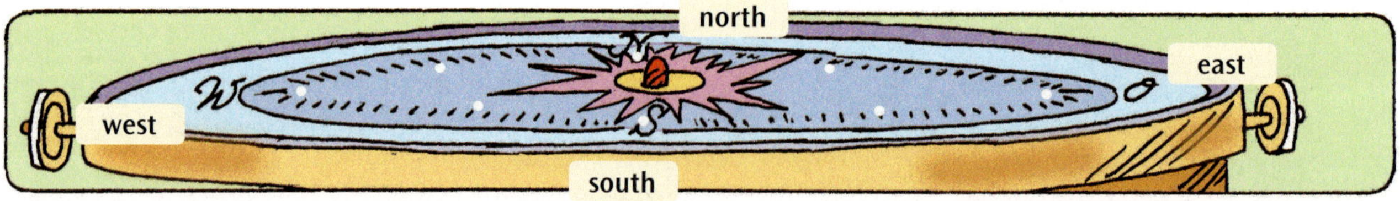

Going This Way and That

Paul is going *up* the stairs.

Judy is running *down* the stairs.

He is going *over* to his neighbour's house.

Peter is just going *out* the door.

Mum and Dad are going *away* for the weekend.

The train is moving *forward*.

In a Hotel Room

- The bed is on the *right* side of the room.
- The table is on the *left* side of the room.
- There are flowers *in* a vase on the table.
- The chair is *close* to the window.

Travel

The Johnsons like *driving*. So when they go on holiday, they take their car and *drive*. Last year they drove all the *way* to Italy. From Britain, it is a long *way* to Italy. On the second day they *arrived* at the border to Italy. From there it was not much *further* to their hotel.

When they *arrived* at the hotel, they checked in.

The hotel was really nice and not *far* from the beach.
They stayed in Italy for two weeks and then *returned* to Britain.

A Directions. Look at a map and fill the gaps with the correct direction.

1 Germany is ______________ of Italy.

2 Ireland is ______________ of England.

3 Wales is ______________ of Scotland.

4 Edinburgh ______________ of Glasgow.

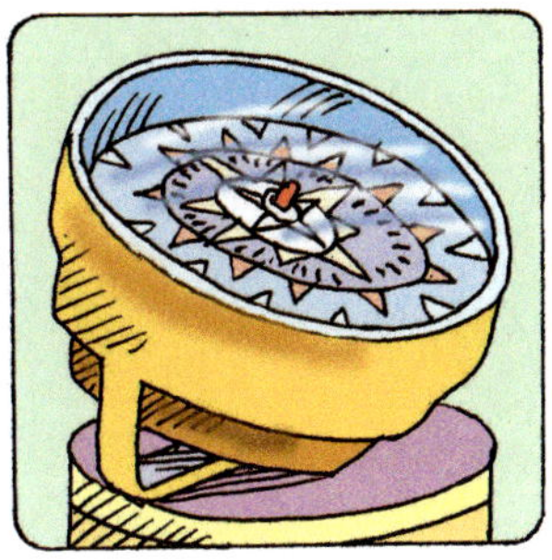

B Prepositions. Fill the gaps with a preposition.

1 The train is leaving. I can see it moving ______________.

2 Lisa's parents are going ______________ tonight but she is staying at home.

3 I would like to sleep now, so please go ______________.

4 Don't run ______________ the stairs. It is too dangerous.

5 When the teacher came into the classroom, everybody had to get ______________.

6 Our neighbours are on holiday. We are going ______________ every day to feed the cat.

C Travel. Replace the underlined phrases with a word from page 24.

1 My parents are planning to <u>go</u> to London <u>by car</u>. ______________

2 They want to <u>come back</u> five days later. ______________

3 But Buckingham Palace is quite <u>a long way</u> from there. ______________

4 I hope that my parents <u>will be here</u> in time for my birthday. ______________

D Places around You. Complete these sentences about yourself. Compare with someone else if possible.

1 My home is close to ______________. I can walk there in five minutes.

2 My home is also not far from (the) ______________. I/My parents can drive there in half an hour.

3 My home is a long way from ______________. I don't go there very often.

4 After school/work, I usually arrive home at ______________ o'clock.

5 When I visit my friends in the afternoon/evening, I usually return at ______________ o'clock.

E Now over to You … Answer the questions using the words from page 24.

1 Describe the position of your home country in the world.
2 Describe your room. Describe where the pieces of furniture are.
3 Did you ever stay in a hotel? Describe the hotel room.
4 Describe the route of the last trip you took.

Maps

- To find out where a country is, you need to look at a *map*.
- The USA can be divided into a *northern* and a *southern* part.
- People in the *south* speak with a *southern* accent.
- Los Angeles is a big city in the *western* USA.
- New York, or the Big Apple, is in the *eastern* USA.

Giving Directions

When you are a tourist, it is good to have a *map*.

But some people also ask for *directions*. A helpful person can *direct* you to the right place.

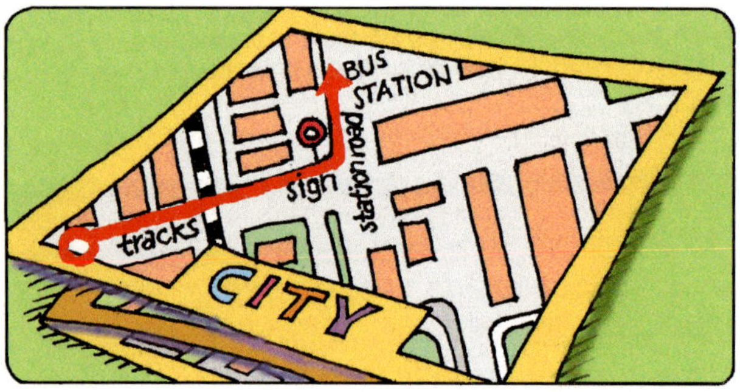

First you cross the railway *tracks*. Then you *turn* left onto Station Road. The bus station is only a short *distance* away, maybe 100 metres. Just follow the *signs*. The station is on the *right*.

Just walk *straight* on for about five minutes. Then walk *through* a park and turn *right*. Now you walk *along* Watson Street. When you are *near* the river, the *museum* is on the *left*.

Going Places

The *library* is easy to find. It is open from Monday *through* Friday. *Access* to the library is *somewhere* by the northern side of the park.

A In the City. Label the pictures with the following words.

post ▪ track ▪ sign ▪ map ▪ library

1 ____________________

2 ____________________

3 ____________________

4 ____________________

5 ____________________

B Word Scramble. Unscramble the groups of letters to fill in the blanks in the sentences.

1 Jenny started driving in the wrong ____________________ TROEDICNI, so she had to turn around.

2 The road did not go any further; ____________________ GARTHITS ahead there was a field.

3 Tim lost his book ____________________ EWHOMERSE in the park.

4 Because of the car accident, a policeman had to ____________________ TREDIC traffic.

C Synonyms. Replace the underlined words with the following words.

access ▪ along ▪ near ▪ right ▪ through

1 There was another <u>entrance</u> for people who had trouble going up the stairs.
2 My house is not on the left side of the street, it is on the <u>other</u> side.
3 It takes me thirty minutes to walk to the store; it is not <u>very close</u> to my house.
4 Walking <u>in between</u> the trees, he found a secret path.
5 He walked <u>next to</u> the river until he came to a park.

D Now over to You … Answer the questions using the words from page 26.

1 How do you get from your home to school, to the park, or to the library?
2 How do you get from the railway station to the nearest hotel?
3 You invited a friend to a party. Explain how to get to your house from where he or she lives.
4 Do you rather use a map or ask for directions?
5 Did you ever get lost? When and where was that?

Traffic

Mr. Smith's *drive* home from work today was awful. First of all, there were just too many *vehicles* on the *road*. Moreover, there was only one *lane* in each direction. At one point, the *railway crosses* over the *street*. Here, the situation was even worse! All *traffic* on the *road* had *to stop* while a long *train* passed. While waiting, one *car* began to have problems. Its *engine* was too hot. This made all the other *drivers* very angry.

Public Transport

- *Traffic* might not be so bad if everyone would *ride* the public *transport*.

- The city is buying more *busses* with the hope that there will then be fewer *cars* on the *road*.

- There are also plans to install more bike *paths* on the side of the *roads*.
- If everyone would take the *bus* or *ride* bikes instead of *driving*, the *journey* home would be much more peaceful.
- Also, with fewer *vehicles* on the *road* there would be less pollution.

Tom Travels to Panama

- During his trip to South America, Tom went on a *tour* of the Panama Canal facility.
- The Panama Canal is a *passage* that connects the Atlantic Ocean and the Pacific Ocean.
- This passage allows *ships* to *travel* quickly from East to West.
- Because of the Panama Canal, ships can *transport* goods across the world faster than if they had to go around South America.
- But not all *ships* use the canal: a *ship* can be either a type of *boat* or an *aircraft*.
- A *boat* is a *ship* that *travels* on water, but an *aircraft* is a *ship* that is capable of *flight*.
- The *route* of an *aircraft* is often more direct than the *path* that a *boat* takes.
- Also an *aircraft* flies at great *speed*. Thus, it is faster to *travel* by plane than by *boat*.

A Means of Travel. Complete the crossword puzzle with the following words.

aircraft ▪ drive ▪ engine ▪ journey ▪ passage ▪ ship ▪ street ▪ train ▪ travels

Across:

1 Paul hates being up high. He only … by train.
2 I took a … in my brother's new car.
3 We arrived at the station late and missed our … .
4 You need to change the oil in the … often.
5 The bathroom is through the first … and on the right.
6 Sarah loves the ocean, but this is her first time on a … .
7 Man's first … to the moon took place in 1969.
8 Please return to your seats. The … will be landing soon.
9 In England, cars drive on the left side of the … .

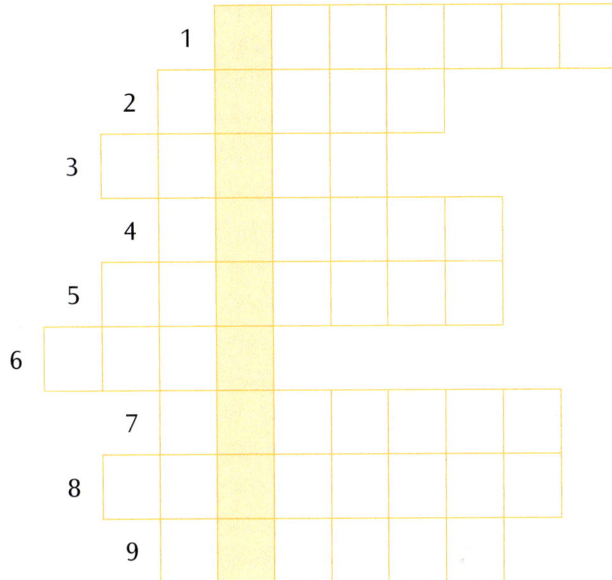

Down: The ____________ of goods is an important area of the economy.

B Odd One Out. Circle the word in each group that does not belong.

1 vehicle – car – path – bus
2 railway – boat – road – street
3 flight – journey – driver – tour

C On the Road. Complete the sentences using the following words.

cross ▪ drive ▪ driver ▪ lane ▪ route ▪ stop ▪ vehicle

1 When you ____________, it is important that you stay in the correct ____________.

2 You should ____________ completely and look both ways before you ____________ another road.

3 It is also a good idea to plan your ____________ before you travel anywhere.

4 A good ____________ will maintain a functional ____________ so as to not put others in danger.

D Now over to You … Answer the questions using the words from page 28.

1 Do you take public transport or drive a car? Describe how people get around in your city.
2 Do you want to go far away on holiday? How would you get there? Would you take a tour while you are there?
3 Describe, in a few sentences, how you would travel around another country.

Whose Is It?

Tom and *his* dog, General, are going for a walk in the park. While there, Tom sees *his* colleague, Mary. This is the first time Tom has seen Mary with *her* dog. General runs over to greet Mary's dog. Tom and Mary start to talk as they watch *their* dogs run around the park.
"It seems that *our* dogs like each other", says Mary.
Surprised, Tom asks, "Is that *your* dog? I did not know that you *own* a dog."
Mary answers, "Yes. That is *my* new friend – I am *its* new *owner*."
Then Tom asks, "What is *its* name?"
Mary responds, "I was thinking of calling it 'Flower'. What do you think I should name it?"
Tom thinks for a moment and says, "I think you should call it 'Tiny'."

Whose idea for a name do you like best?

The New Guitar

When his grandfather died, John *acquired* a valuable Les Paul electric guitar. Now he wants to play it. First, he needs to learn how to play. He decides to *pay* his musician neighbour Chris for guitar lessons. Chris suggests, "You do not want to break such an expensive instrument! You should *buy* a cheap guitar to learn with." John does not want to *spend* a lot of money on a cheap guitar. Chris says, "Sometimes a store will have a *sale*, when you can get a good instrument for a lower price. Or try looking at a used instrument store. They *sell* instruments for very little money."

For Your Eyes Only

This file is for your eyes only. The information in it is *private*.

The public is not allowed to walk on this piece of land. It is *private property*.

"The money is *due* on March 3rd. Please make your *payment* before this date."

Your Own Business

Linda recently started her *own* business. She *owns* a store that *sells* pet supplies. As the store *owner*, Linda has a lot of *expenditures*: things that she must *spend* money on. For example, she must make sure that there are things in her store for people to *buy*. She wants *to acquire* products that will interest her *consumers*: the people who *own* animals. To help with her expenditures, Linda went to a nearby bank to *obtain* a *loan*: money that she can borrow from the bank and pay back in the future. In order to receive the *loan*, Linda had to give some *personal* information to the bank; such as her name, her date of birth and her address.

A Whose Is It? Complete the sentences using the following words.

her ▪ his ▪ its ▪ my ▪ your ▪ our ▪ their

1 My neighbours have a dog. I cannot sleep at night, because ______________ dog is so loud.

2 Annie has a red dress. It is ______________ favourite dress.

3 John bought a book about Rome. I would really like to borrow ______________ book.

4 I have a mountain bike. Everyone really likes ______________ mountain bike.

5 We are getting married. Will you come to ______________ wedding?

6 Do you have a mobile phone? What is ______________ number?

7 The cat sleeps over there. ______________ bed is in the corner.

B Buying a New Car. Complete the sentences using the following words.

due ▪ loan ▪ owner ▪ pay ▪ payment ▪ spend

Mary wants to be the ____________[1] of a shiny new car, but she does not have enough money. She needs a ____________[2], so that she can afford one. The bank manager told her that she can only ____________[3] €3000 and that she needs to ____________[4] €150 each month for two years. The ____________[5] is ____________[6] at the beginning of each month.

C Hard Earned Money. Complete the sentences using the following words.

acquired ▪ consumer ▪ expenditures ▪ own ▪ personal ▪ sale ▪ whose

1 In a capitalist economy, businesses compete with each other for the money of the ______________.

2 The professor asked his students to write an essay about their ______________ spending habits.

3 Do you rent your house, or do you ______________ it?

4 Jenny has many things to buy each month. Her ______________ include: rent, telephone and food.

5 Mark is a poor student. He only buys clothes when they are on ______________.

6 Jane found money on the kitchen table, but did not know ______________ it was.

7 The company is in serious trouble. Over the last three years, it has ______________ too much debt.

D Now over to You … Answer the questions using the words from page 30.

1 Have you ever been to a market? Describe the activities that go on there.

2 Do you have a large family? Maybe you have a lot of friends. Who belongs to whom? Describe the relationship between your family members or the family members of your friends.

3 Do you own anything? Is it something that everyone knows about or do you keep it a secret?

Cash and Credit

With *money* you can buy things. There are many forms of *money*, including coins, paper bills, and credit cards.

A *bank* is a type of business. People put their *money* in a *bank* to keep it safe.

Cash is *money* that exists as paper bills and as coins. You can withdraw *cash* from a *bank*.

The *money* used in the United Kingdom is called the British *pound*. A *pound* is also a measurement. One *pound* is about 0.45 kg.

Something is *expensive* if it costs a lot of *money*. Something is *cheap* if it costs very little *money*.

Doing Business

Mrs. Smith is a musician. She also has the *trade* of building musical instruments. Mrs. Smith builds instruments that make beautiful music. She *produces* instruments of very high quality. Because Mrs. Smith is a musician, she knows what a good instrument is. Her knowledge of music is an *asset* – something that she owns and can use to make *money* in the future. Mrs. Smith has her own *business* where she builds instruments. She also wants to *open* her own *store* where she can sell her instruments. Her *store* will be a small *shop*. A *shop* is another word for a small *business*. Mrs. Smith will be her own boss, so she will not have to deal with any corporate *management*. The instruments that she produces are her *products*. She will sell her *product* at her new shop. Mrs. Smith's instruments *cost* a lot of *money*, but the instruments do not *cost* her a lot to make. Her costs include materials and time. Because the instruments are *cheap* to build but *expensive* to buy, Mrs. Smith hopes to *gain* a large *profit* from her instruments. The *income* Mrs. Smith earns from selling her product will pay for her costs. Some of the *income* will not be used. Mrs. Smith will use the extra *money* as *capital* to help her *business* to grow. Mike would like to buy an instrument from Mrs. Smith, but he does not have enough *money*. He cannot *afford* Mrs. Smith's high *prices*. Mike will try to *deal* with Mrs. Smith. Mrs. Smith is willing to sell her instruments at a lower *price* to people who show real interest in her *products*.

Peter Buys His First Car

- Peter has just received his driving licence. Now he wants to buy his first car. Peter is not *rich*, so he cannot buy an *expensive* car. He does not want a *cheap* car either, because he is afraid that a car with a low *price* will not run right.
- Peter is *shopping* for a car with a good *value*: one that is reliable and fun, but one that does not *cost* too much. He decides to look for a used car.
- Peter goes to a used car dealer, a *company* that sells used cars. Peter looks at the *price* of each car to see if he can *afford* it. Finally, he finds a car that he can *afford* to buy with the *money* he has. The dealer asks him if he wants to *trade* in his old car for the newer one. Peter answers that this is his first car, so he has nothing to *trade*.
- The dealer gives a *bill* to Peter that shows the amount that he needs to pay. The *bill* shows the *price* of the car and some *fees*: additional costs that Peter needs to pay. She asks Peter if he is buying the car with *cash* or on *credit*. If he pays *cash* he will need to pay the whole *price* now, but on *credit* means he can pay a smaller amount each month for several years.
- Peter feels that he got a good *deal* on the car.

A Looking for a Deal. Complete the sentences using the following words.

afford ▪ cash ▪ cheap ▪ cost ▪ credit ▪ expensive ▪ money ▪ open ▪ price ▪ rich

1 Mary does not like to spend a lot of ______________ on food.
She is always looking for the best ______________ on the things that she buys.

2 She says, "Shopping at the supermarket is too ______________ for me.
I cannot ______________ the high prices that the supermarket charges for its products."

3 Tom suggests going to the open market, "If you are not ______________ and don't have a lot to spend, the open market is the place to go."

4 "When it is compared to the supermarket, the open market is ______________."

5 "For example, the same fruits and vegetables ______________ less at the open market."

6 But Tom offers a reminder, "At the open market, you cannot use ______________ cards to pay for what you are buying; you can only pay with ______________."

7 "And the open market is not ______________ every day."

B Stock Market Research. Complete the sentences using the following words.

bank ▪ business ▪ fee ▪ pound ▪ produces ▪ product ▪ trade ▪ value

1 Dr. Jones is an economist. He studies changes in the ______________ of different currencies – the variation in how much one type of money is worth in a different type of money.

2 He explains that many countries have a central ______________ that issues the country's money.
People use the money when they purchase things.

3 For example, in Britain the money is called the ______________.

4 The value of one type of currency depends a lot on what its country ______________.

5 The currency itself is also a ______________ of a country, because it can have value in another country.

6 Some international banks are in the ______________ of exchanging currencies from different countries.

7 For example, if you are travelling to Britain, you can ______________ euros for pounds.

8 The bank makes money by charging a ______________ – a small amount that you pay for the bank's service.

C Now over to You … Answer the questions using the words from page 32.

1 What has more value to you, expensive things or cheap things, and why? How do you usually pay when you buy something? Where do you prefer to shop, at big stores or small shops, and why?

2 Where do you (or does someone you know) work? In a large company or a small shop? In what role? Describe the job.

Shopping

Three for the price of one. This is a good *deal*!

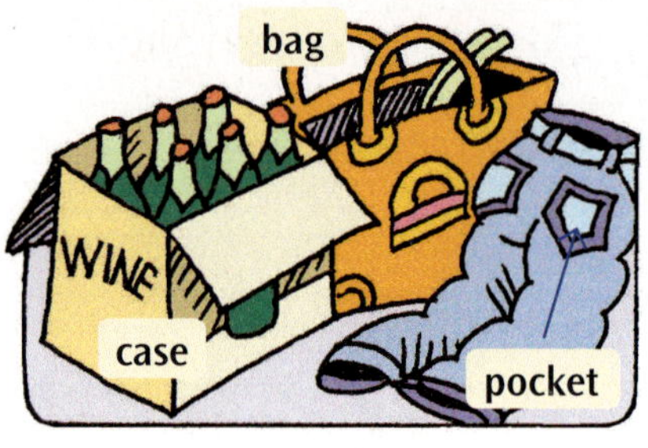

Buying and Selling

- Someone who buys items or services is a *client* or a *customer*.
- A place where people can go to buy things is a *store*.
- Sue bought a dress, but it is too small. She goes back to the *store* to *exchange* it.
- A commonly-accepted style is a *fashion*. New clothes are often presented at a *fashion* show.
- If you spend more money than you have, you are in *debt*.
- When a *shop* sells a *product* they should make a *profit*.
  That means they should get more than they paid for the *product*.

Business and Enterprise

- A supermarket needs fresh *supplies* several times a week.
  If you do not like to go shopping, you should have a *supply* of food at home.
- All the items a *shop* has is its *stock*. If something is not to be found in the *shop*, they might still have it in *stock*.
- A *company* organized to make money is an *enterprise*. You can also call it a "business".
- When you sell your *products* in a *shop*, it is a *commercial* enterprise. You expect to make a *profit*.
- A really big *company* or a group of *companies* is called a *corporation*.
- The *distribution* of aid *supplies* can be a quite difficult in Third World countries.
- Often, the aid *supplies* need to be *delivered* by airplane.

Shops and Stores

- When a *shop* is not open, it is *closed*. Some *shops close* at lunch time but most are open all day.
- Lisa always *shuts* her door behind her. She does not like open doors.
- The manager of a *shop* makes decisions and takes care of the employees.
- She has to *manage* different sections of the business.
- Some *companies supply* other *companies* with the things they need. Food *companies supply* food to restaurants.
- Jenny decided to *wear* a new dress for the job interview, so she went to the *store* to buy one.
- When you have a job interview you should *dress* well. It makes a good impression.

A Shopping. Find six words from this chapter in the word search.

C	R	P	A	S	Z	I	Z	S	M	X
U	U	O	V	A	T	R	U	T	A	L
B	O	C	A	B	V	B	C	C	N	C
M	A	K	O	S	I	R	I	O	A	H
C	H	E	N	H	E	R	P	R	G	E
E	N	T	E	R	P	R	I	S	E	R
F	A	T	B	E	L	I	W	F	L	C
T	E	H	H	A	K	N	E	U	E	H
D	U	T	Y	S	P	G	A	I	T	F
T	R	A	N	Q	U	O	R	O	N	E
D	E	L	I	V	E	R	K	H	I	G

B Managing Supply Distribution. Complete the sentences using the following words.

corporation ▪ customers ▪ deliver ▪ distribution ▪ managing ▪ wear

John works for a huge supermarket _______________1. He is in charge of _______________2 several employees. Because of his responsibilities, John is supposed to _______________3 a suit to work. John plans where to send all the supplies by making a _______________4 map. By looking at the map, the employees know where to _______________5 the supplies. So each day, the _______________6 at the supermarkets can buy fresh food.

C Money Matters. Match the words with their definitions or descriptions.

1	to close → d	a	customer
2	a profit	b	something having to do with making money
3	a client	c	a good price
4	a deal	d	to shut something
5	commercial	e	the money made by selling something

D Shopping for Clothes. Complete the sentences using the following words.

dresses ▪ exchange ▪ fashions ▪ look

Before Mary buys new clothes, she looks in magazines for the latest _______________1. She likes to look pretty when she shops, so she _______________2 up in her nicest clothes. Mary goes to many different stores, always trying to find a new stylish _______________3. Sometimes Mary makes a mistake and buys the wrong size. If so, she takes the item back to the store and asks to _______________4 it for another size.

E Now over to You … Answer the questions using the words from page 34.

1 Do you like shopping? What kind of things do you like to shop for? Where do you buy them?
2 Do you or someone you know have a job in a store? Describe what you do, what the other person does.

The Body

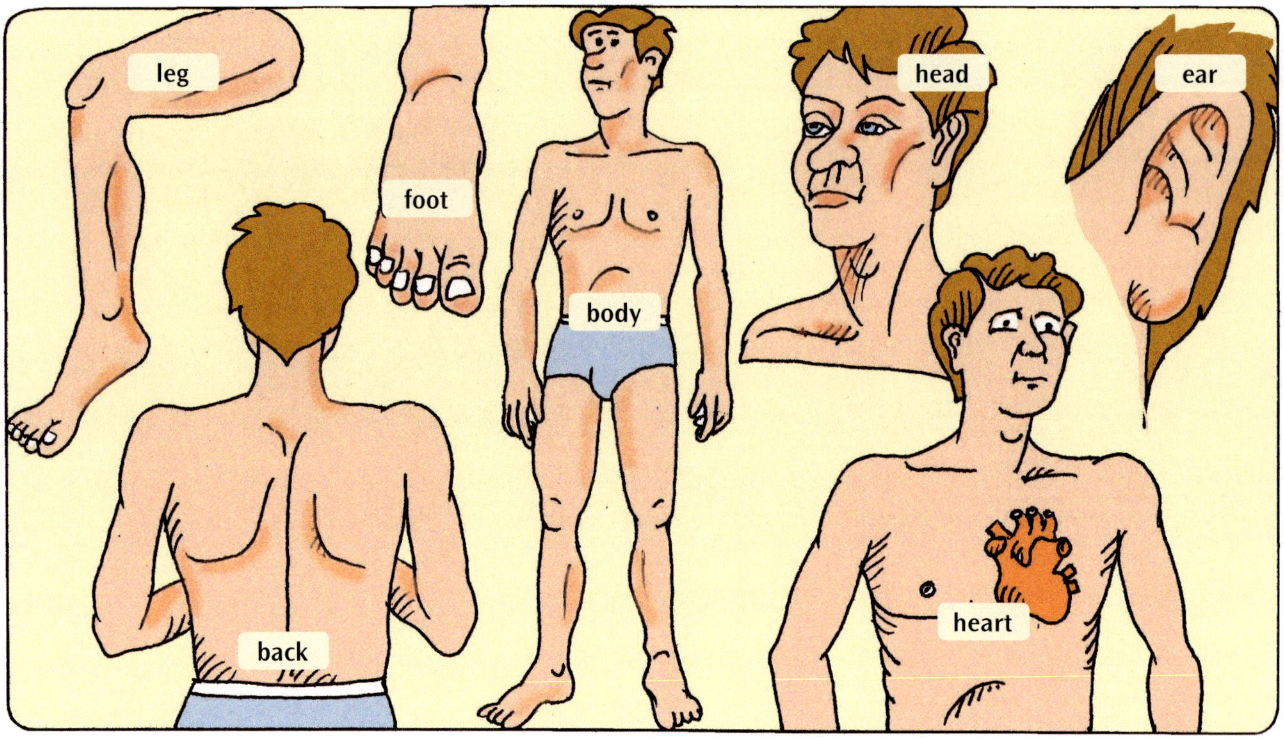

The Face

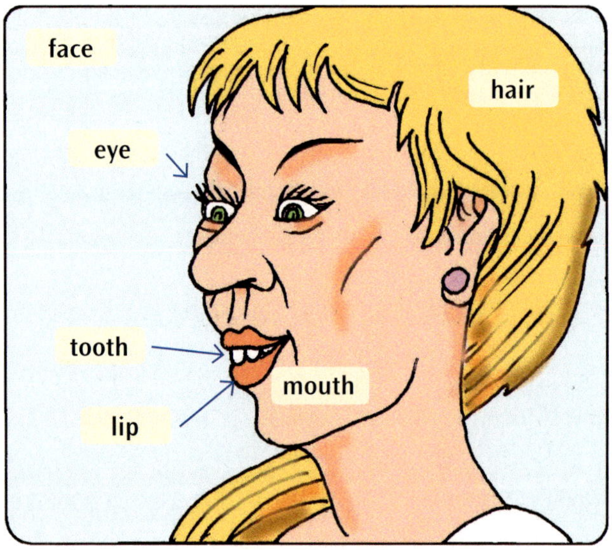

Neck and Arm

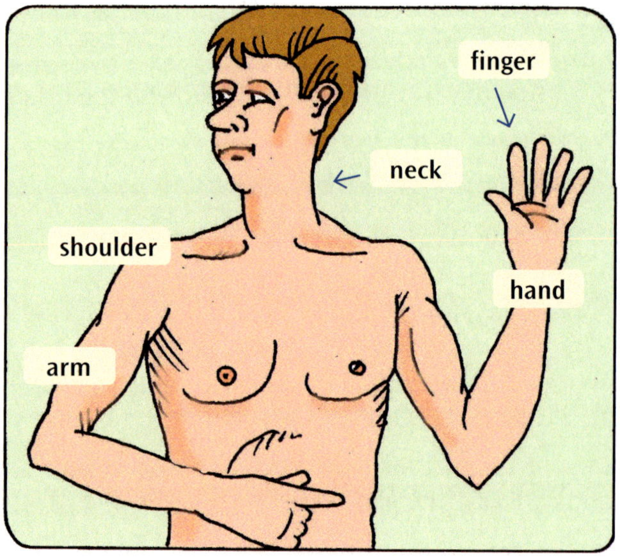

Our Body

- Inside our *head* is the *brain*. We use our *brain* to think. Animal *brains* are smaller than human *brains*.
- Every night we go to bed to rest our *bodies*. An average human *sleeps* seven to eight hours a night.
- Our *skin* is the largest organ of our *bodies* and covers us almost completely.
- There are about five to six litres of red liquid in our *body*.
  Blood is needed for the transport of oxygen from the lungs into all *body* parts.
- Jenny likes to sing. She has a beautiful *voice*.
- George is a couch potato. He needs more *physical* activity in order to stay healthy.
- Susie fell on her *arm*. She injured the *joint* between her *hand* and her *arm*.

A Parts of Our Body. Label the pictures with the following words.

mouth ▪ eye ▪ hair ▪ ear ▪ lip ▪ tooth ▪ blood ▪ shoulder ▪ finger ▪ heart

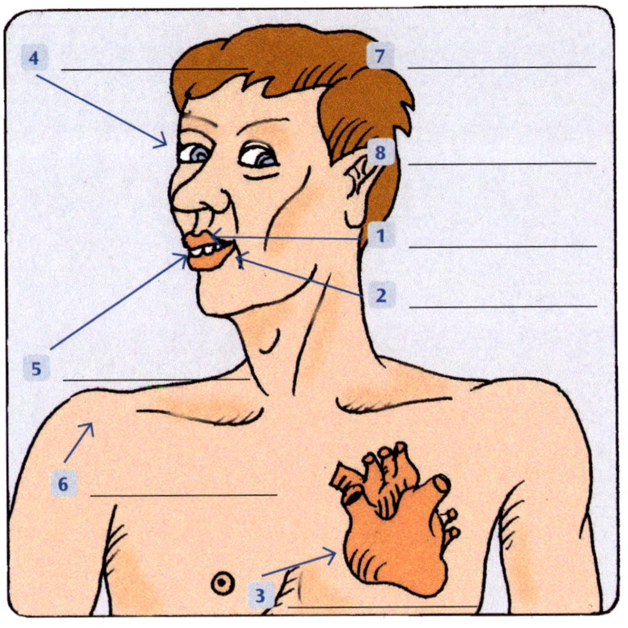

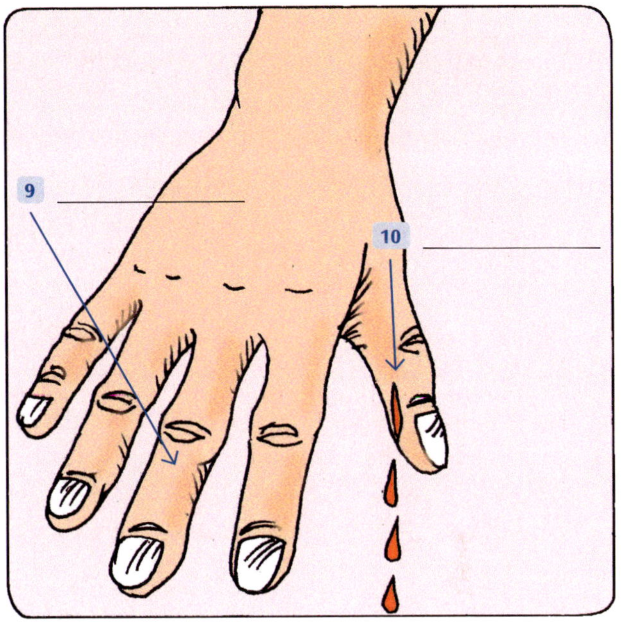

B Our Body. Draw a stickfigure and label the following body parts.

head ▪ neck ▪ arm ▪ hand ▪ leg ▪ foot

C A Hard Day. Complete the sentences using the following words.

sleep ▪ voice ▪ skin ▪ back ▪ physical ▪ joint ▪ brain

1 George sits at an office desk every day. He needs to improve his __________ fitness. So he goes jogging.

2 The students in the classroom were very loud, so I almost had to shout. At the end of the day I had lost my __________.

3 Tina gets up at 5 am every morning. She goes to bed at 9 pm because she needs to __________ for eight hours.

4 There was no bus, so I had to carry my baggage for a mile. Every __________ of my body hurts now.

5 My teacher used to say, "Please, use your __________ to think!"

6 My chair at work is uncomfortable. It hurts my __________ if I sit in it too long.

7 Sue sat in the sun for too long. Her __________ is all red and burnt.

D Now over to You … Answer the questions using the words from page 36.

1 What do you look like? Describe yourself for someone who cannot see you.
2 Which parts of the body do you use most in the job you do? What do you use them for?
3 What do you do to stay physically fit? What should everybody do to stay healthy?

An Accident

The *accident* was really bad, but luckily nobody *died*. All the passengers of the car *survived*.
One person suffered a serious *injury*. Michael's arm and face were *bloody* and the *pain* in his leg was terrible.
The ambulance took him to the hospital, where he received *medical treatment* for his *injuries*. Michael was lucky: he only *suffered* some *cuts* and a broken leg.
Nevertheless, he needed an *operation* to fix his leg. After the *operation*, Michael had to stay in hospital for a week to *recover*. While he was at the hospital, he was *treated* with antibiotics to prevent infection.

In the Hospital

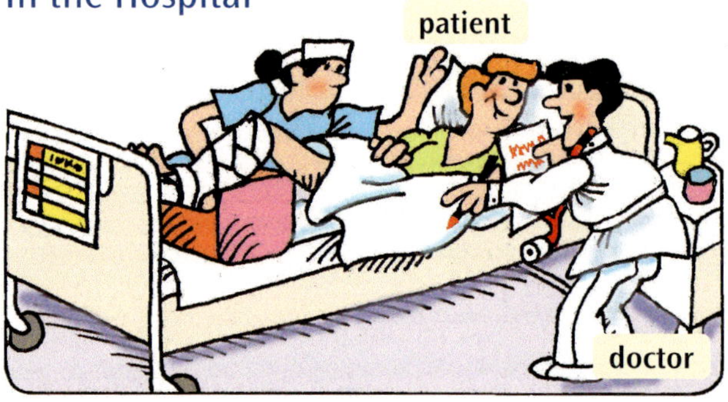

- The doctor told John to *rest* in bed for a few days.
- The nurse took good *care* of the patient.

When Grandpa Died

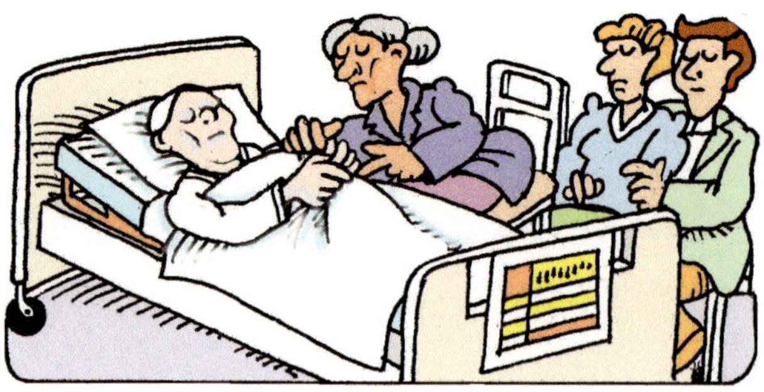

- His wife and family were with him when he took his last *breath*.
- He *died* peacefully after a long illness.
- His family is very sad about his *death*.

Going to the Doctor

- When you are sick and want to go to the *doctor*, you need to call and make an *appointment*.
- If you are ill or injured, you need to get medical *treatment*. Doctors learn at the university which *treatment* is right.
- If a person's heart stops working, he will *die*. The heart is a *vital* organ.
- *Drugs* are supposed to help the *patient*. A common *drug* against pain is aspirin.
- Aspirin provides *relief* against headaches and pain.
- With some *diseases* you must go to the *doctor*, but with others you usually get better after a while.

A Mark's Accident. Complete the sentences using the following words.

accident ▪ appointment ▪ bloody ▪ doctor ▪ injury ▪ operation ▪ pain ▪ rest

1 This morning, Mark had a bad ______________: he fell down the steps in front of his house.

2 He thought he had broken his nose, because his nose was all ______________.

3 All the blood made his friend Jenny think that Mark's ______________ was serious.

4 So Jenny took Mark to the ______________ to get medical treatment.

5 Since it was an emergency, Mark did not need an ______________ to see his doctor.

6 The doctor said Mark's nose was not broken, so no ______________ would be necessary.

7 But Mark's head hurt really badly. The ______________ was terrible.

8 The doctor told Mark to take some aspirin and ______________ for a few days.

B Odd One Out. Circle the word in each group that does not belong.

1 relief – treatment – to recover – death
2 doctor – injury – nurse – patient
3 to help – to treat – to care – to hurt
4 dad – death – die – dead

C Mrs. Smith's Serious Disease. Complete the sentences using the following words.

breath ▪ die ▪ disease ▪ drugs ▪ medical ▪ suffering ▪ survive ▪ vital

1 Mrs. Smith was infected with a dangerous virus that caused a severe ______________.

2 She was in a lot of pain and had a high fever. She was ______________ from very serious symptoms.

3 The virus had infected her lungs. Mrs. Smith's chest hurt with every ______________.

4 The virus was also attacking other ______________ organs, like her heart and her brain.

5 Her family was really afraid that she was going to ______________.

6 While in the hospital, Mrs. Smith received excellent ______________ treatment.

7 Mrs. Smith's doctor gave her efficient ______________ to fight off the disease.

8 After three weeks in the hospital, he told her family that she would ______________ the disease.

D Now over to You … Answer the questions using the words from page 38.

1 Have you ever had an accident? What happened? Did you have an injury? Did you need an operation? Who took care of you?
2 Have you ever been sick? What was the treatment? How long did you have to rest?
3 Describe your last medical visit. Who works at the office where you usually go? Did the doctor suggest that you take any drugs? How did the drugs help you?

In the Kitchen

Doctors Recommend

Good *food* is essential for a healthy *life*. Here are a few things that you can try: it is better to *eat* five small *meals* each day than two large *meals*. Instead of going to a *restaurant* for *lunch*, make your own *lunch* before you go to work. If you like a big *dinner*, eat it early not right before you go to bed.
Most doctors recommend that you *drink* a glass of milk every day. *Tea* or fruit juice are healthier *drinks* than cola, which contains a lot of sugar. Some doctors also say you should not have more than one alcoholic *drink* per week.
But it is not only what you eat and drink that is important: good *health* requires physical exercise. Get your children in the habit early: *feed* them healthy food and encourage them to play outside.
By following this advice, you and your family will *live* a long time and have healthy *lives*.

A Bad Cut

Maria *cut* her finger with a knife.

The *acid* from the lemon made the *cut* hurt really badly.

It was necessary to clean the *cut*. In order to prevent infection the *cut* has to stay *clean*.

A Good Health. Complete the sentences using the following words.

clean ▪ cut ▪ food ▪ health ▪ life ▪ live ▪ restaurants

1 It is important to get physical exercise and to eat healthy ______________.
2 Tom died at 95, after living a long and happy ______________.
3 Some people say that it is healthier to ______________ in the countryside than in the city.
4 Peter is sick all the time. He has very poor ______________.
5 Do not eat that off the ground! It is not ______________.
6 Peter does not like to cook. Instead, he goes to ______________ quite often.
7 A dull knife might slip and ______________ you instead of the bread.

B On the Table. Create a Picture. Draw images and label them using the following words.

bottle ▪ plate ▪ cup ▪ glass

C Drinks. Complete the sentences using the following words.

acid ▪ coffee ▪ drink ▪ tea ▪ wine

1 The juice of a lemon contains a lot of ______________.
2 In Asia, there is a long history of people using ______________ as a kind of medicine.
3 Some people think that drinking a glas of red ______________ every day is healthy.
4 Many people drink ______________ in the morning, either with milk or black with sugar.
5 There is nothing better than a cold ______________ when you are thirsty on a hot day.

D Eating and Drinking. Organise the following words into the three categories below. Can you add more words for meals, or nouns and verbs that are connected with food?

eat ▪ dinner ▪ drink ▪ feed ▪ food ▪ lunch ▪ meal

verbs	nouns	meals

E Now Over to You … Answer the questions using the words from page 40.

1 What do you like to drink? Are there drinks that go better with a certain meal than others? Describe what you drink during the day.
2 Is a healthy life a happy life? What do you do to stay healthy?
3 Imagine that you are eating a nice breakfast with your family. Describe what you see on the table.

Physical Activity

In the Garden

Movement

Moving Out

Chris is going to Paris for half a year. Before leaving his apartment in London he has to *clear* out his room. He also needs to *spread* some cloth over the valuable furniture. He *marks* all things that need to be taken to the neighbour, such as his plants. Before leaving, he *leans* against the wall and stares at his favourite painting. He decides to *cover* it with cloth, too. Even though Chris would like to stay, he rings at his neighbour's door and *hands* him the key to his apartment.

A Physical Activity. Label the pictures with the following words.

to blow ▪ to carry ▪ to pick ▪ to pull ▪ to push ▪ to shake ▪ to stick

B At the Airport. Complete the sentences using the following words.

covers ▪ hands ▪ leans ▪ removes ▪ sits ▪ stand ▪ walks

1 Mary __________ to a nearby café as she waits for her flight to Berlin.
2 Mary, Susan, and Annie __________ in line. They need to show their tickets.
3 On the plane, Annie __________ down quickly in her window seat.
4 Then Annie __________ back and closes her eyes. She does not like flying.
5 She __________ her ears with her hands and takes a deep breath.
6 After some time, her friend Susan __________ Annie's hands from her ears and tells her that everything is fine.
7 Susan __________ her friend a cup of tea and they both enjoy the flight.

C Synonyms. Replace the underlined words with the following similar words.

clear ▪ climbing ▪ lie ▪ slips ▪ staring

1 Mark was so impressed by the girl on the other side of the room that he could not stop <u>looking</u> at her.
2 Mark does not feel well. Therefore, he decided to stay at home and <u>rest</u> on the sofa.
3 The road is covered with ice. Chris can't do anything as his car <u>slides</u> down the hill.
4 <u>Going</u> up the Himalayas requires a lot of experience and energy.
5 After the party Chris had to <u>remove the dishes from</u> the table.

D Now over to You … Answer the questions using the words from page 42.

1 Do you like outdoor activities or sports? Tell someone what you like to do.
2 Do you like gardening or working outside?
3 What are your favourite activities, what do you not like?

Opposites

When the *light* is on, the room is bright. When the *light* is off, the room is *dark*.

Hot water can be dangerous. *Hot* is the opposite of *cold*. Ice is frozen water. It is *cold*.

The sofa is very *soft*: It is comfortable to sit on. A rock is *hard*. Some people prefer *hard* chairs to *soft* sofas.

Sensation and Perception

- When the dogs come out of the water they are wet. When the water is all gone, they are *dry* again.

- A fire is *hot*. It gives off *heat*. But during a *hot* summer the *heat* can be too much.
- A *fresh* apple comes right from the tree. *Fresh* fruit is good for your health.

- Some people like it *quiet* when they have to concentrate.

- When learning to walk, babies must learn to keep their *balance*.

Verbs of Sensation

- You can *hear* many different sounds and noises in a big city. You use your ears to *hear*.
- When you *listen*, you pay attention to what you *hear*. Kids should *listen* to their teachers in class.
- Put a shell up to your ear; the shell *sounds* like the ocean.
- When you *touch* something with your hand, you can tell if it is *hot* or *cold*.

More about the Senses

- *Sight* is the *sense* that allows us to see. Without *sight*, one cannot read normal books.
- A *sound* is something you can *hear*. There should be no loud *sounds* in the library.
- A *noise* is a *sound*. If a man tripped and dropped his books in the library, the *noise* would make a lot of people pay attention.
- The *ring* is the *noise* a phone makes when someone is calling. Most cell phones now have a lot of different *rings*.
- Something that is *sharp* can cut. *Sharp* knives should not be in the reach of small children.
- Most people like *warm* weather. *Hot* weather can be a problem, especially for older people.
- Through our *senses* we *hear*, see, smell, taste, and *touch*. A dog's *sense* of smell is much better than a human's.
- Some people feel under *pressure* during tests. If there is too much *pressure* they might fail.
- He could tell by her *tone* of voice that she was very angry. Her *tone* became more aggressive by the minute.
- *Silence* is the absence of *sounds* or *noise*. Sometimes when people have a lot of stress, they need *silence*.

A Noises in the Dark. Complete the sentences using the following words.

warm ▪ hear ▪ hot ▪ dark ▪ noise ▪ sharp ▪ cold

During the night, a ______________ [1] woke John up. He got out of his ______________ [2] bed and quickly put on some clothes so he would not be ______________ [3]. Although the house was ______________ [4], John tried to walk around without turning on a light. He thought he could ______________ [5] someone in the kitchen. In the hall he hit his knee on a chair and felt a ______________ [6] pain. Then he opened the door to the kitchen. "Dad!" John's son Michael said, "Do you want to drink some ______________ [7] chocolate? It will help you to get back to sleep."

B Odd One Out. Circle the word in each group that does not belong.

1 to hear – to sound – silence – noise
2 to listen – noise – quiet – dry
3 balance – dark – cold – hard
4 heat – hot – to touch – quiet
5 hard – ring – tone – noise

C Making a Mind Map of the Senses. Add the following words to the body parts. Can you find more words to add to the mind maps?

listen ▪ hear ▪ sound ▪ noise ▪ sight ▪ touch ▪ feel ▪ see

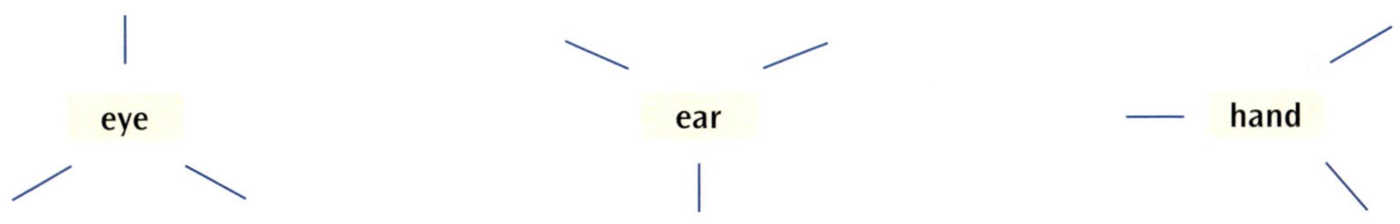

D Something Is not Right. Correct the following sentences.

1 The five senses are to hear, to see, to taste, to smell, and to eat.
2 The room is dark when the light is switched on.
3 Too much pressure makes students feel relaxed and will help them to pass their exams.
4 The tone of her voice was aggressive. So he thought she was happy.
5 My phone has a low ring now. I changed it because I could not hear it when I was in another room.
6 I bought some bananas before I went on vacation. They are quite fresh now.
7 Most sofas are hard, but chairs are usually soft.
8 Before I go to bed, I turn on the heat because I like it cold.

E Now over to You … Answer the questions using the words from page 44.

1 Do you like to go to the beach? What can you hear, see, feel, touch, and smell at the beach?
2 What about the city? What different sensations from the beach can you find in the city?
3 What sense is most important to you and why? Are there sensations that you do not like? What are they and why do you dislike them?

Moving up and Down

The starter *raises* a flag. The hot air *lifts* the balloon and it begins to *rise* into the sky.

John *throws* the paper airplane across the room. The paper airplane *flies* fast.

Bob *dropped* a cup again. He needs to be more careful. He is always *dropping* things. Brenda *fell* and broke her arm last week.

A Trip to London

Mary promised to *send* Paul a post card from England. She is excited about *riding* the London Underground. Paul gave her some good advice, "Be careful on the platform, so the train does not *hit* you when it arrives. When you *enter* the train, you need to 'mind the gap'. This warning reminds you to *step* onto the train carefully. There are many Underground lines and sometimes you have to *transfer* from one train to another. To make a *transfer*, step off the train and find the platform for your next train. Often, it is only a short *walk* away. Stay with the *flow* of people as you walk to your transfer platform. Do not be too *slow*: You need to *move quickly* or else you might miss your train. You'll know if this happens, because you will see the train *disappear* into the tunnel. If this situation *arises*, do not worry. You can always *jump* on the next train."

A Jumping Rabbit

When a rabbit *jumps*, it makes many quick *movements* with its legs. Jane is a physicist. She wants to study rabbits in *motion*. She has a slow-*motion* camera to capture all the *action*: from the time when the rabbit decides to *jump*, through the rabbit's *rise* into the air, and to its fall back to the ground.

A Odd One Out. Circle the word in each group that does not belong.

1 rise – lift – raise – drop
2 action – silence – movement – motion
3 sit – walk – step – move

B Crossword Puzzle. Complete the crossword puzzle with the following words.

enter ▪ flows ▪ jumped ▪ motion ▪ move ▪ send ▪ throw ▪ transfer

Across:
1 The rocking of a boat on the sea is a … that makes me sick.
2 The river is dry; no water … in it anymore.
3 The table is very heavy. I cannot … it.
4 You can smell the flowers when you … my garden.
5 The dog … over the gate and ran away.
6 Sarah will … me a text message if she is late.
7 Paul is going to the bank to … money to his account.
8 Keep the city clean. Please … your waste in the garbage.

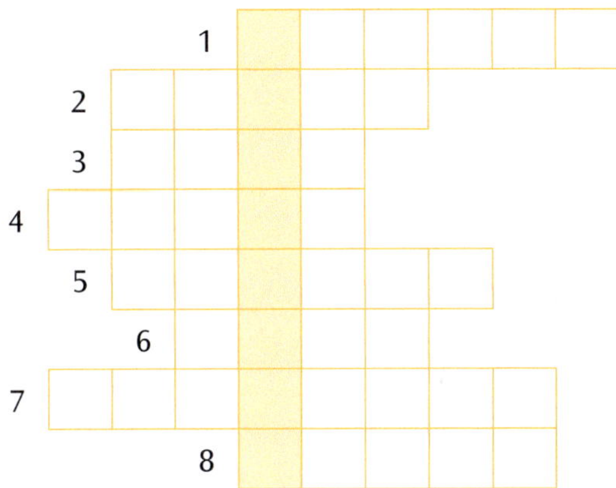

Down: The students want to join a ________________ to stop global warming.

C Stock Exchange. Complete the sentences using the following words.

fell ▪ quick ▪ rise ▪ transfer

1 This morning, there was a ____________ in the price of oil.
2 Many shareholders made a ____________ decision to buy as much shares as possible.
3 But by the end of the day, the price of oil ____________ again.
4 In the end, many people lost money in this ____________.

D Making Mind Maps for Movement. What can you ride? What can fall? What can (you) fly? What can rise? Use words from page 46 and add more words you know.

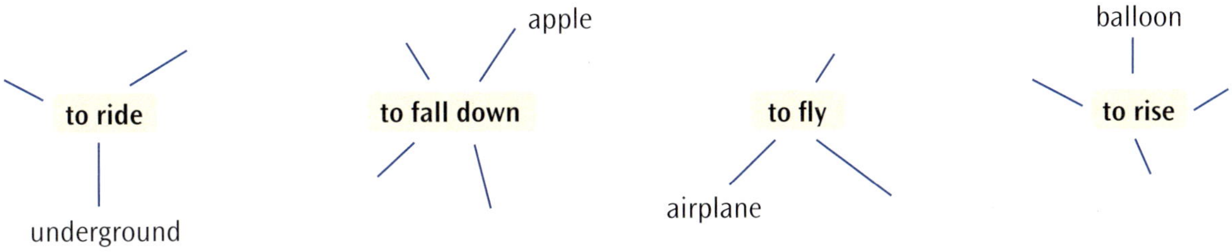

E Now over to You … Answer the questions using the words from page 46.

1 Would you rather ride a bus or walk? Describe your favourite way of transport or travel.
2 Have you ever played with a paper airplane? Describe what you do with it and what it does on its own.

Feelings

A *smile* is the easiest way to show that you are *happy*. Most babies *smile* when they see their mothers.

When we are *sad*, *tears* come from our eyes.

Are you *afraid* of ghosts? We *fear* things that we cannot see or do not understand.

Perception

Runners have to be able to run *fast* to win races. *Rapid* steps allow a runner to move faster.

Most people like houses or apartments with a nice *view*.
From this window you have a wonderful *view*.

The present Jane received for her birthday was a *surprise*.
Another *surprising* thing was that her friends had organized a birthday party.

A *shot* coming from a gun makes a loud noise.

Susan found out, after her *fall*, that she had broken her arm.

Lisa's Future

Lisa is a sales person in a big department store and she *worries* about her future. She thinks about it constantly. She wants to make progress in her job. But it is hard to *advance* in your job if you do not have special training. Lisa *hopes* that extra training will help her become manager one day. She has really set her *mind* on it and it is her greatest wish. The *reason* is that she wants to have responsibilty and earn more money. She cannot *bear* the thought of staying a sales person for the rest of her life. She has a *feeling* that she will be really *happy* once she has a better position. As a manager, it will be a *pleasure* to go to work in the morning.

Movement and Perception

If you put a ball at the top of a hill, it will start to *roll* down to the bottom.

People *laugh* when they hear something funny.

John's mother could not *remember* where she had left her keys.

A Positive or Negative Feelings? Do you associate positive or negative feelings with the following words? Arrange them into two lists.

to smile ▪ to worry ▪ sad ▪ shot ▪ fall ▪ to laugh ▪ tears ▪ pleasure ▪ fear ▪ surprise ▪ happy ▪ afraid

positive	negative

B What People Feel. Complete the sentences using the following words.

shots ▪ reason ▪ view ▪ remember ▪ rolled ▪ fast ▪ surprise ▪ mind ▪ pleasure

1 Peter was such a ______________ runner that no one could beat him.
2 The sound of gun ______________ every night made Annie worry about the safety of her area.
3 Jane said the ______________ why she had to leave class early was to go to work.
4 The ____________ from the top of the building was everything Mark had hoped: he could see the whole city.
5 Starting at the top of a hill, the young child ______________ down to the bottom, and stood up, unable to walk straight.
6 Michael was unable to hide his ______________ when his wife unexpectedly brought him lunch at work.
7 Because Tom had hit his head so hard, he could not ______________ what had happened.
8 "It was a ______________ to meet you," said Ron as he shook Lisa's hand.
9 Paul could not understand Susan's tears; he had thought in his ______________ that everything was okay between them.

C Feelings. Do you think these sentences are true or false? Rewrite them to make them true, from your point of view.

1 Being happy is a good feeling.
2 When someone has hope, they fear that something might happen.
3 People always smile when they are afraid.
4 Laughing is a good way to show that something is funny.
5 Most parents do not worry about their children.

D Now over to You … Answer the questions using the words from page 48.

1 What makes you happy? Describe a time when you were happy. What had happened?
2 Most people are sad or worried sometimes. What makes you sad or worried and why?
3 What were you afraid of when you were a child? Are you still afraid of it?

The Mind

Peter received a *notice* from his mother.
It read: "Do not *forget* to feed the cat."

At the book store, Linda *discovered* an old book.
As she began reading it, her *mind* drifted out of *reality* and she began to *imagine* strange creatures.

Cause and Effect

- Seeing the desert was a great *experience* for young George. He had never *experienced* anything like it before.
- Without thinking about the risk, Paul climbed the highest mountains. When he woke up in the hospital, the *thought* came to his mind: "I should have been more careful."
- The price of oil influences our economy in a strong way. The use of alternative energy would reduce this *influence*.
- Jane lost her *memory* completely in the accident. Slowly, she began to *remember* some things. When she left the hospital her *memory* was fully restored and she could *remember* everything.
- I *wonder* who will win the football match next week. It is a wonder our team won last week, since three players are injured.

Realising Your Mistake

Mary is afraid of her father's *reaction* to finding out that she was in a small car accident. She takes a moment to *reflect* on the situation that led up to the accident: The motorcycle in front of her was flashing its left turn signal, but Mary *ignored* this and tried to drive around the motorcycle. Then the motorcycle started to turn and hit the side of her car. She *realises* now that she made a big mistake by not waiting for the motorcycle to turn. After seeing the damage, she thinks maybe her father will not *notice* the scratches on the car door. To Mary's *knowledge*, there might have been scratches there before, but she is not certain about that. She *imagines* how disappointed her father would be if he found out that she had not told him the truth. Ultimately, she decides that the most *reasonable* action is to tell her father about her accident. In the future, she will *watch* what other drivers are doing more carefully.

Judging Thoughts and Actions

- Mark should *concentrate* on learning instead of thinking about his girlfriend all the time. He thought so much about her that it was difficult for him to *concentrate* during exams.
- When I met my father at the station, I did not *recognise* him at first. He had only seen pictures of me, so he did not *recognise* me either.
- Some diseases are *serious* threats. If a doctor says a disease is *serious*, the sick person may not live.
- It is hard to *assess* whether Lisa will win or lose the game. Seeing her strong opponent, she *assessed* her own chances as low.
- The newspaper article *revealed* the details of the actor's wedding. It also *revealed* that his new wife had been a dancer in a club for a long time.

A Reality and Imagination. Unscramble the groups of letters to form the words described in the sentences.

1 TONIEC __________________: information written on a piece of paper

2 NLFECNIUE __________________: another word for 'effect'

3 NDMI __________________: where thinking takes place

4 CORITANE __________________: what follows an action

B Gaining Knowledge. Replace the underlined words with the following opposite words.

forgets ▪ reality ▪ serious

1 My grandmother is 99 years old. This is why she always <u>remembers</u> my name.
2 The president announced that terrorists posed a <u>silly</u> threat to people travelling abroad.
3 Journeys to distant planets could become <u>fiction</u> in a few years.

C Becoming Experienced. Replace the underlined words with the following similar words.

discovered ▪ reasonable ▪ wonder

1 When Paul cleaned his room, he <u>found</u> the old disc he had been looking for, for so long.
2 Your father's advice sounds <u>appropriate</u> to me.
3 Every time I see a plane in the sky I <u>ask myself</u> how a big thing like that can possibly fly.

D Action and Reaction. Complete the sentences using the following words.

experience ▪ ignore ▪ realises

1 It is difficult to describe the feeling of love. You have to ____________ it yourself.

2 Michael loves to play football. But as he gets older, he ____________ that he cannot run as fast as he used to.

3 You would not call them best friends. Each time they meet they simply ____________ each other.

E Training Your Memory. Match the words with their definitions or descriptions.

1	to estimate	a	reveal
2	to focus your mind	b	recognise
3	to already know something because of an experience in the past	c	assess
4	In the best reports, secret agents … important secrets.	d	concentrate

F Now over to You … Answer the questions using the words from page 40.

1 Under which circumstances can you learn and concentrate best?
2 Comment on the importance of knowledge in your life. What do you do to gain knowledge?
3 Describe your favourite methods to train your memory.
4 Describe the influence of imagination on your daily life. Explain the term 'daydreaming'.

Images of Perception

Because Ron is not very tall, it is hard for him to *reach* things up high.

Even though the door was locked, the thief was able to *force* it open.

Mrs Blenman cannot understand how she lost her keys, since she *recalls* putting them in her bag.

It was hard for the boy to decide which ball he wanted, but he finally *selected* the blue one.

While the girl was sleeping, she had a *dream* in which she was a queen.

Each year, Ron *receives* a present for his birthday.

Preparing for University

Ever since she was young, it has been Sarah's *desire* to go to university. She knew that there are many *requirements* for attending university, such as good grades and strong recommendations from her teachers. Having *satisfied* these requirements, she is ready to start her studies next semester.

Going to University

Now Sarah is looking for a place to live. She found out that student housing is always in high *demand*, so there is very little chance that she will be able to live there. Therefore, it is *necessary* that she finds an apartment some place else in the city. There is an apartment not far from the library, but the rent price *concerns* her. When she *estimates* how much she will be able to spend each month, she decides that, in order to make it work, she will need to *seek* out a roommate to share the cost. Then she remembers the deposit. Now she *wishes* that she had saved more money from her summer job.
Sarah does not want to *impose* on her parents, but after coming to the conclusion that there is no other way, she decides to ask for their help. She explains her *need* to borrow money from them for the deposit on her apartment. She is grateful when her parents say they can lend her the money and assures them that she *intends* to pay all of it back next summer when she gets another summer job.
September comes and classes begin. Sarah did not realise how much *mental* energy is required to stay focused in her classes and on her homework. She feels like her brain needs a break from all the thinking. She was a good student before and liked the *recognition*. She also wants to *maintain* her good grades at university. The courses at university are harder than the ones in school, so she has to learn new ways to *cope* with a heavy work load. She studies her notes after every class so that she can *retain* the information better and remember it for the final test.

Sarah's parents are proud of how well she does in her first semester, but they also see how tired she is. They *press* her to come home for the holidays. At first, she thinks she does not have time; she needs to prepare for the next semester. In the end, Sarah agrees to go home for one week to visit her parents. She realises that constant work is not a good thing; a healthy mind *requires* rest and relaxation.

A Odd One Out. Circle the word in each group that does not belong.

1 dream – desire – to impose – to wish
2 to impose – to press – to force – to receive
3 desire – need – necessary – requirement
4 requirement – demand – to force – to wish
5 mental – to recall – to estimate – need

B Achievements and Improvements. Complete the sentences using the following words.

force ▪ estimates ▪ satisfied ▪ mental ▪ intended ▪ recall ▪ necessary ▪ recognition

1 The child is a genius; his ____________ skills are far better than those of most children his age.
2 John was not ____________ with how his drawing turned out, so he decided to start over.
3 Eggs are a ____________ ingredient for this recipe. Otherwise, the cake just will not come out right.
4 Mrs. Jones gave special ____________ to the one student, by telling the class that she had no mistakes on her test.
5 The weather forecast ____________ that there is a 50% chance of rain today.
6 Paul knew that he had a doctor's appointment on Friday, but he could not ____________ what time it was at.
7 Sometimes parents ____________ their kids to do what they do not want to do.
8 Mike ____________ to help his mother clean the house, but he got home after the work was done.

C Word Search. Find the following words in the word search.

concern ▪ cope ▪ demand ▪ dream ▪ expect ▪ maintain ▪ need ▪ require ▪ retain ▪ select

A	M	A	I	N	T	A	I	N	R
H	Z	K	B	R	D	H	D	E	Z
C	C	O	N	C	E	R	N	E	G
D	O	F	C	D	R	F	Z	D	D
R	P	W	Z	F	S	W	K	O	R
E	E	K	R	E	Q	U	I	R	E
T	A	I	K	F	I	T	G	L	A
A	E	D	E	M	A	N	D	H	M
I	D	S	S	E	L	E	C	T	D
N	N	O	P	E	X	P	E	C	T

D Now over to You … Answer the questions using the words from page 52.

1 What are your wishes and dreams? What are some things that you need?
Describe how you would like your life to be.
2 What did your parents ask you to do that you did not like? Did they demand it or did they ask nicely?
3 Have you ever had to make a tough decision? Describe what it was.

Professions and Titles

The *farmer* is in the field gathering hay for his horses.

The *captain* steers the ship carefully down the river.

Our tour *guide* in London told us a lot of interesting facts about the city.

Mrs Connor works as a *secretary* making appointments and taking phone calls.

At this point of the process, a *worker* takes the separate parts and creates a finished product.

Company Roles

- George and his band are looking to hire an *agent* to help them get a record contract.
- After he finishes his studies in economics, Mike plans to *apply* for a job at a bank.
- The hospital has just hired a new *specialist* who will perform brain surgery for the medical clinic.
- The railroad workers fought for better pay, but the company's *executives* would not give in.
- Dr. Jones is recognized internationally as an *expert* on how to build environmentally friendly houses.
- After Peter helped his company win the contract, his *employer* gave him a substantial bonus.
- As a border control *officer*, it is Officer Smith's duty to make certain all passengers show their passports when they enter the country.
- Dr. Peterson is *chief* of staff at the hospital. He is in charge of ensuring that all the necessary hospital positions are filled.

A Tough Situation

After a year of low profits, the company *chairman* has gathered the other *directors* at a *meeting*. He tells them that the company is in trouble. They need to *create* more income. "We need to *plan* for the future," he says. He wants the directors to work with the business *managers* to develop new *projects* that will help turn the failing company around. He wants to get everyone involved: "I want every *employee's* input on this. I want to see every worker talking to his *colleagues* about ideas that we can use." The chairman offers hope, saying, "I think we will find something of value if everybody *applies* himself to coming up with a useful solution."

Building Procedures

- The city council has a *plan* to build a new town hall in the city center.
- An architectural firm has created a *design* of the new building called a 'blueprint'.
- The rest of the work is then divided into *tasks*. These smaller jobs add up to complete the whole project.

A Corporate Ladder. Complete the sentences using the following words.

to apply ▪ captain ▪ executive meeting ▪ secretary ▪ plan

1 Linda is bored by her current job. She wants _______________ for a new one somewhere else.

2 The thief's _______________ seemed perfect, but as he came out of the bank the police were already there.

3 The boss criticized Ron's work harshly during their _______________.

4 When Timmy grows up, he wants to be the _______________ of a big ship.

5 Mary needs an appointment to see Dr. Jones, so she will call his _______________.

B Different Jobs. Assign a job to each of the following images.

1 _______________ 2 _______________ 3 _______________ 4 _______________

C Different Occupations. Complete the crossword puzzle using the clues provided.

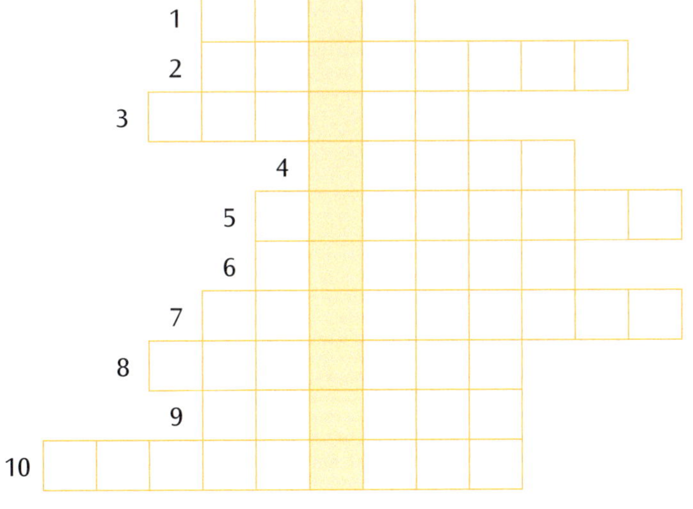

1 A small division of a large project is a(n) … .
2 The person who offers work is a(n) … .
3 Someone who knows a lot is a(n) … .
4 Another word for 'main' is … .
5 A company can have more than one … .
6 A person who works in the field.
7 A person who works in the same office is a(n) … .
8 A person who works for the police or border control is a(n) … .
9 An architectural firm creates the … of a new building.
10 The president of a company is called the Chief … Officer or CEO.

A person who has special training in an area is a(n) _______________.

D Now over to You … Answer the questions using the words from page 54.

1 Have you ever tried to get a job? What were the steps that you had to take to get it? Describe who you talked to and what they requested from you.
2 If you could have any job in the world, would you be a simple farmer or a rich executive? Describe your dream job.
3 As a young child, what did you want to be when you grew up and why?

An Important Meeting

Paul loves his job; he works in a firm that *designs* advertising campaigns for other companies. He has a big meeting this afternoon to discuss the *release* of a new product. The company wants to *launch* their new product in one year. Today there is a *planning* meeting where Paul will give a presentation. The presentation will reveal the *marketing* ideas Paul has developed to help sell the company's product. His plan is to *promote* the new product so that consumers will be interested in buying it. Before the meeting, Paul reviews his notes to *prepare* for the presentation. He *checks* to make sure he has everything he needs. Paul hopes to convince this *panel* of important people that he has the best ideas.

Organisation in the Office

- Employees often find themselves to be so *busy* with their work, that they do not have time to *organise* the things in their office.
- When employees get behind on organisation, cleaning up an office can seem a difficult task to *undertake*.
- Ideally, workers should spend a little time every day to *arrange* their workplace and sort through their paperwork.
- Many workers find it helpful to keep their important papers in a *file*.
- *Files* that are in order are an efficient *reference* system, because employees know where to find the documents they need.
- Having an organised workspace helps maintain a *professional* atmosphere where employees can work effectively.

A Sweet Job

Yesterday, Amy's teacher gave an assignment to the students to learn about what their parents do for work. The students should visit their parents at work and *conduct* an interview with their parents. Once the bell rang at the end of class, the teacher *released* the class to go home. Later that night, Amy tells her father about the assignment. He invites her to come to work with him the next day.

Mr. Jones is Amy's father. He works at a candy factory. Every day at the factory, the workers gather an *arrangement* of ingredients that go into making a certain type of candy. The workers pour these ingredients into a machine that mixes them together to create the raw candy. Next, the raw candy goes into the machine that Mr. Jones *operates*. This machine presses the raw candy into a large, flat sheet. After that, another worker uses a sharp *tool* to cut the candy sheet into bite-size pieces. The manager then takes one piece as a *sample* and eats it to see if it tastes right. Sometimes the candy does not taste good because there is an issue with the ingredients. When this happens, the manager will *appoint* a worker to find out what the problem is and fix it. Mr. Jones's factory only wants to sell candy that tastes good.

A A Battle at Court. Complete the sentences using the following words.

appointed ▪ arrangement ▪ conduct ▪ organised ▪ release ▪ working

1 The court room has a good seating ____________ that allows everyone in the room to see the judge.
2 The accused man could not afford a lawyer, so the judge ____________ a lawyer to defend him.
3 The lawyer will not ____________ any information regarding his client.
4 The State does not yet have a ____________ theory that explains how the crime occurred.
5 The judge asked the police to ____________ an investigation into the cause of death.
6 Outside the court house, individual people ____________ themselves into an angry crowd.

B Keeping on Top of Things. Complete the sentences using the following words.

busy ▪ checks ▪ file ▪ panel ▪ tool

1 In today's meeting, the ____________ will decide if it accepts the business proposal.
2 Michael keeps important letters in the red ____________.
3 In most businesses, the computer is now a necessary ____________ because it has so many functions.
4 At work, Jane was already too ____________, but then her boss gave her even more work to do.
5 Every morning when Peter gets to work, he ____________ his phone to see if there are any messages.

C A Day at Work. Complete the sentences using the following words.

arranged ▪ marketing ▪ operate ▪ order ▪ prepare ▪ professional ▪ reference ▪ release

1 Some computers do not have enough memory to run the programs, so they __________ very slowly.
2 Peter asked his old boss if he could use her as a __________ when he applies for a new job.
3 Jill's boss is usually very patient, but when he is under a lot of stress, he starts to __________ people around.
4 John will print off his work history and review possible interview questions to __________ for his job interview.
5 The agency has designed a __________ plan that involves both television and internet advertisements.
6 At the end of the quarter, the company will __________ its performance information to the public.
7 The law firm asks its employees to wear suits in order to create a __________ atmosphere.
8 Mary __________ to have both meetings today, one right after the other.

D Now over to You … Answer the questions using the words from page 56.

1 Do tools help you get the job done? Describe some of the equipment you use at work.
2 What role do you play at work? Describe what you do in your job.
3 Are you orderly or messy? Describe how you organise your work world.

Work Places

a *farm*

a *firm*

a *factory*

an *office*

A Strike in the Factory

Peter went to university and works in an *office* now. He started a *career* as a manager. Peter takes care of the *employment* needs of the *factory*, by hiring and firing workers, and by negotiating the *wage* that a worker is paid. One day Peter wanted to increase the *revenue* of the *factory* and reduced the *wages* of the workers. The workers, who have to do the hard physical *labour* in the *factory*, were not happy about Peter's decision. The *labour* union told them to stop working. So they went on *strike*. Peter said he would just *employ* new workers. Because the workers were afraid of losing their *jobs*, they went back to work.

The World of Work

- George *worked* hard to save money for his trip around the world.
- Linda wants to *earn* more money, so she asked her boss to increase her wage.
- A lot of people have difficulties finding a *job*. The *unemployment* rate is really high right now.
- The various *mechanisms* of the economy are difficult to understand.
- In order to be competitive, the *firm* had to invest in new *equipment* and technology.

Dream Jobs

- Of all *departments* Anne likes the sales *department* best. After ten years of working in the sales *department*, Anne became the executive.
- Having finished school, Peter enrolled for pilot *training*. He dreams of being a pilot one day.
- John sent over fifty *applications* before he finally found a *job* as an architect.
- Linda's *function* as a manager is to order supplies for the workers.
- Lisa works as a secretary. After work, her eyes hurt from looking at the computer *screen* all day long.
- Paul has a good understanding of technical functions, so he decided to study *engineering*.
- Mark's English is really good. Therefore, his boss always sends him to the international *conferences*.
- George and Paul *displayed* their new machine at the convention. A lot of managers were interested in buying it.

A Where Do You Work? Unscramble the groups of letters to form the words described in the sentences.

1 MRIF ________________: another word for company

2 CFFOIE ________________: another word for bureau

3 FCTORAY ________________: another word for plant

4 TMNERADPET ________________: a section within a company

5 RMAF ________________: a work place in agriculture

B Business as Usual. Match the words with their definitions or descriptions.

1	the condition of being out of work → d	a	conference
2	another word for income	b	application
3	to receive or gain something in return for work	c	training
4	another word for occupation	d	unemployment
5	a course for a special exercise	e	equipment
6	an official and written request for something	f	to earn
7	instruments or machinery that is needed for something	g	wage
8	to show something you produce	h	job
9	a meeting where people discuss certain things	i	to display

C People and Their Jobs. Complete the sentences using the following words.

career ▪ employ ▪ employment ▪ engineering ▪ function ▪ labour ▪ mechanisms ▪ revenue ▪ works

George is a good manager. He ________________ 1 a lot, sometimes even on the weekends. The company's ________________ 2 rose after George changed its marketing strategy. If George ever leaves, the company will have to ________________ 3 a new manager that can do everything he does.

Paul is a construction worker. It is a job that requires a lot of physical ________________ 4. He would like to find a type of ________________ 5 that is less physically demanding. Since he likes to build things and is very talented at drawing, he is thinking of pursuing a ________________ 6 as an architect.

Peter studied mechanical ________________ 7. Now he works at a company that produces vital ________________ 8 that run the life support systems on the space station. The ________________ 9 of these systems is to provide oxygen and warmth to the space station modules, so that the astronauts can live safely in space.

D Now over to You … Answer the questions using the words from page 58.

1 What kind of field do you work in? If you don't have a job yet, where would you like to work?
2 Do you prefer physical work or working in an office? What kinds of equipment do you use?
3 Describe how you got your last job. Did you have to go through specific training?
4 How do you prepare for a job interview?

Winner Takes All

Annie, Mary and Mike are having a *competition*. Annie *missed* the target. Mary was *successful* and hit the centre of the *target*. Mike is *ready* to shoot.

The Oscar is a famous *award*.

Tim has *strong* muscles. But his real *strength* is his will to *win*.

Competition on the Tennis Court

George and Mary both play tennis. Last Saturday they played a match. Mary plays tennis really well. She has not *lost* a game in a whole year. After George and Mary shook hands, they *faced* each other and started the game. George really wanted to *win*. He played well – he really *fought* – but he did not *achieve* his goal: he *missed* too many balls and *lost*. Even though Mary *won* again, George was not mad that Mary had *beaten* him. He agreed that she is a very good tennis player and plays tennis on a higher *level* than him. But George is determined not to give up. He will *attempt* to *beat* Mary in the next match.

Failure and Success

- Employees should be given the *chance* to prove that they can do a good job on difficult projects.
- Some companies give their employees social *benefits*. For example, they help to pay for their health insurance.
- The boss of the company has more *power* than an employee.
- Jane's project was a *success*, she *won* a prize and gave an interview to a newspaper which likes to publish *success* stories.
- Mr Doyle is Peter's boss and is usually against his ideas. But today he was not in *opposition* to his new project. On the contrary, he happily agreed!
- At the end of the year the company realised that the red toothpaste did not sell nearly as well as they had hoped. This project was a complete *failure*.

A In the Work Place. Complete the crossword puzzle with the following words.

opposition ▪ level ▪ competition ▪ power ▪ strong ▪ target

Down:
1 When two people fight each other, they are in a … .
2 If you have big muscles, you are … .
3 The high or low status of an employee in a company is also called a … .

Across:
4 Something you aim at is a … .
5 You have to have … to be able to lead a country.
6 … makes it harder to succeed. You have to convince the people who are against you.

B Puzzle Work. Unscramble the groups of letters to fill in the blanks in the sentences.

1 My bags are packed and I am ________________ AEYRD to go.

2 George is a good tennis player, but Mary is ________________ TEBERT.

3 If I can earn an "A" in the class, I will consider it a ________________ CSCESUS.

4 My teacher has given me one more ________________ ECCNHA to take the test.

5 Because John was so smart, it was always a ________________ TIFENBE to study with him.

6 Mary always ________________ ETTTMAPED to get to class on time, but she was often late.

C Odd One Out. Circle the word in each group that does not belong.

1 to achieve – to lose – to win – to beat
2 strong – best – successful – failure
3 opposition – strength – to win – award
4 power– to beat – to lose – to fail

D Now over to You … Answer the questions using the words from page 60.

1 Have you ever been in a competition?
2 What kind? Who won and who lost and why?
3 If you were to win an award today, what would you do to celebrate?
4 Describe a project you worked on.
5 Was it a success? If yes, why? If no, why not?

Sports and Competition

- Jenny likes to *run*. At the competition she *ran* as fast as she could and came in first place.
- It is hard to *win* a competition if your opponent is very *powerful*.
- The coach *threatened* to throw Mary out of the team if she would not practice twice a week with the others.
- At the football match last weekend Chris failed to *score* a goal and his team lost one to two.
- Who will *succeed* in winning the race?

Work or Play

Objective is another word for aim or goal. The *winner* receives the first prize. It was a big *challenge* for Paul to *run* the 42 km race. After their *victory* against the German football team, the Italian team celebrated all night.

Science and Development

- To *develop* means to advance, to grow or to design something. Albert Einstein was one of the first *scientists* who successfully *developed* a theory about the speed of light.
- To *examine* is to look at or consider something carefully. Before selling aspirin for the first time, the *scientists* had to *examine* its effects on the human body carefully.
- To *result* means to be produced or to happen as an effect of something. Back pain can be the *result* of too much hard work.

Science and Technology

- Physics is a field of *science* that studies how things move.
- A *theory* is the *result* of a lot of research. Darwin is known for his *theory* of evolution.
- An *analysis* is a type of *research*. An *analysis* of the dirty water showed that it was poisonous.
- The *model* of the machine illustrates how it is actually working.
- The professor introduced a new *method* to analyse radiation.
- We analysed the *structure* of the rock formation.
- The new *data* give us information on how to improve the correctness of the *experiment*.
- A new *theory* formed the *basis* of our work.
- His *source* of knowledge was his books.

Science and Concepts

- We found that smoking was an important *factor* for the risk of a heart attack.
- A special procedure for the *experiment* is written down in a detailed *scheme*.
- You should understand the *concept* of the *theory* if you want to use it in your essay.
- Copper is a *medium* that can transport electricity.
- Doctors follow the *principle* that life is worth saving.
- If you mix a *base* into an acid, the result will be a weaker acid.
- The students had difficulties finding the *solution* to the professor's question.

A Odd One Out. Circle the word in each group that does not belong.

1 winner – to run – victory – to succeed
2 method – scheme – medium – concept
3 result – effect – solution – objective
4 powerful – to threaten – to result – to score

B At the Laboratory. Match the words with their definitions or descriptions.

1	data	a	is the examination of something
2	science	b	is the arrangement or composition of different parts that make one whole
3	an analysis	c	is an invitation or request to compete in a contest
4	the structure	d	is the organised and systematic study of knowledge
5	a challenge	e	is an element or force that influences the result of something
6	a factor	f	are facts, figures or information

C Categorising Scientific Terms. Organise the following words into three categories based on their common meaning.

principle ▪ to examine ▪ source ▪ basis ▪ model ▪ to research ▪ to develop ▪ theory ▪ base

D Word Search. Find seven words from this chapter in the word search.

S	E	V	F	N	T	C	K	T	T
O	W	I	N	N	E	R	G	F	G
L	F	C	X	V	E	V	J	U	V
U	J	T	H	E	O	R	Y	V	C
T	X	O	C	X	D	E	V	M	O
I	K	R	G	J	C	S	M	R	N
O	I	Y	F	T	V	U	E	C	C
N	T	C	F	J	V	L	F	V	E
C	E	F	F	E	C	T	X	H	P
I	L	F	E	A	Q	M	H	K	T

E Now over to You … Answer the questions using the words from page 62.

1 Have you ever been in a competition? Were you successful? Why did you win or lose?
2 Describe a project that you worked on. How did you organise it? Did you use a specific theory?
3 Are you a competitive person? What has been your biggest challenge? Which factor helped you in the competition?

School and University

At *school*

In Mrs. Brown's *class* the *pupils* learn to read and write.

At the *university*

Dr. Smith is *observing* the temperature during the *experiment* and notes the results in a *table*.

Dr. Berman's Course

Dr. Berman is a specialist for biology at the *university*. In his *course* his *students* have to *observe* the behaviour of dogs. Then the *students learn* to describe their *observations* with *scientific* terms. As a final project the *students* in Dr. Berman's *class* had to design their own *experiment*. Some *students observed* how music affects the behaviour of dogs. For the final presentation they *generated* a table showing their results.

Lisa's Studies

After finishing High *School* Lisa wanted to become a doctor. She applied for medical *school* and began her *studies*. In her first year she had to take three *modules*: 'Chemistry 1', 'Blood Systems' and 'The Brain'. Lisa was surprised by the *difficulty* of the chemistry *course*. The *professor* told her that she needed a lot of *practice*. Lisa really wanted to *pass* the *course* and worked hard, but in the end her grade was not good enough. After she got an 'F' and *failed* the *course* for the second time, she changed her *subject*. For her new *subject* she chose English and now wants to become an author.

Better Education

The *staff* is a group of people who work together in one institution. The five *professors*, the teaching assistants and the two secretaries make the *staff* of the German Department. They have a *staff* meeting every Monday.
The *education* you get at *school* is very important. After *school* many people continue their *education* at a *university* or *college* and then get a job.
The department's new international *science* program was a *creation* of the new department head. The *staff* of the department is very excited about the *creation* of this new program.
The teaching assistants have to go through training again as a *consequence* of the new program. It is much more demanding than the old one.

A Studying the Sciences. Find the following words in the word search.

difficulty ▪ generate ▪ learn ▪ module ▪ observe ▪ scientific ▪ studies ▪ university

D	I	M	L	E	N	U	N	O	S	O	T
M	O	D	U	L	E	C	H	W	B	G	E
S	E	I	F	L	P	V	N	S	E	Y	T
T	R	F	Q	T	R	A	E	T	E	G	A
U	S	F	T	B	D	R	I	E	S	Z	R
D	L	I	E	A	V	R	N	X	U	N	E
I	S	C	I	E	N	T	I	F	I	C	N
E	N	U	I	U	V	G	E	D	R	S	E
S	S	L	E	A	R	N	S	I	I	T	G
A	Y	T	R	K	S	T	L	J	N	E	R
S	T	Y	T	I	S	R	E	V	I	N	U

B Classes at the University. Replace the underlined word with the following words.

classes ▪ failed ▪ observations ▪ staff ▪ student

1 Paul noticed a lot of interesting facts in class, so the professor thanked him for his <u>remarks</u>.
2 Every professor in the department was asked to come to the <u>employee</u> meeting with the department head.
3 Each <u>person</u> in the class was asked to choose a project to work on.
4 Jenny had two <u>courses</u> on Mondays and Wednesdays.
5 Because Ron <u>did not pass</u> his English test, he had to take the same course again.

C Formal Education. Complete the sentences using the following words.

course ▪ education ▪ experiment ▪ pass ▪ school ▪ scientist ▪ subjects

1 Annie told everyone that she liked her literature ______________ best because she likes to read.

2 The ______________ wrote instructions on how to mix the chemicals for the experiment.

3 In order to record the results the students have to observe the ______________ very carefully.

4 Mark's favourite ______________ were English and Biology.

5 Peter was able to ______________ the class by getting an 'A' on the test.

6 When Mary turned five, she started going to the local ______________.

7 To improve his ______________, George signed up for an evening class in math.

D Now over to You … Answer the questions using the words from page 64.

1 What kinds of school did you attend? At what age did you go to which school?
2 Who were your favourite teachers? What did they teach and why did you like them?
3 Did you ever have difficulties in a class? What was the problem?

School and Education

At the *college*

A *test*

Study Time

- At the end of the semester, Paul has to take an exam. In order to pass it, he has to *study* a lot.
- Mary is not doing very well at school. Her *teacher* told her that she needs to *improve* her grades.
- Susan needs more *discipline*. She goes to the cinema rather than doing her homework.
- After weeks of taking extra *classes* in English, Jenny got an 'A' on her last essay. She has shown a lot of *improvement* in speaking and listening.
- At the end of the *school* year, the *students* take final *examinations* to show what they have *learned* during the year.
- Unfortunately, Mark made a lot of *mistakes* on the math *test*. He *failed* the *test* and had to take it again.

Teachers at Work

- *To teach* is to give somebody lessons. The *professor teaches* English to the *students*.
- *Instruction* is another word for lessons or *teaching*. Mary needs *instructions* on how to do the experiment.
- *To train* is to give somebody lessons in a skill or profession. The hairdresser *trained* his new assistant to cut hair.
- The *class* trip to the museum of science was very *educational*. After the trip most *pupils* were much more interested in *class*.
- Before *students* can take an advanced language *course* they need to take an *assessment test* to find out whether the *course* is appropriate for them.
- Every day the *professor* checks his *students' presence* in *class*. It is important that everybody is there before he starts.
- Peter's *concentration* while he was doing homework was so intense that he did not hear the phone ringing.

At College

- A *degree* is a title received for having finished *school* or a *course* of *study*.
  After four years of *studying* History, Mary received a *degree* in History.
- After finishing six years of *university*, Chris will receive his *master's degree*.
- He is applying for a *teaching* job at a small *college* in Wales now.
- An *institute* usually belongs to a *university* or a *college* and does a special kind of work.
  The *Institute* of Biology is well-known for its research projects.
- A *grant* is money that you receive and that does not have to be paid back.
  The government offers *grants* to *students* who cannot afford to pay for *university*.

A Life on Campus. Assign each of the following words to the picture or fill in the blanks.

concentration ▪ discipline ▪ master's degree ▪ professor ▪ students ▪ teaching

1 ______________________

2 ______________________

3 John is working really hard to receive his ______________________.

4 A lot of ______________ is necessary when you are taking exams.

5 John is lucky: Mary is ______________ him what he did not understand in class.

6 One day John hopes to be a ______________ himself.

B A Normal Day at School. Unscramble the groups of letters to form the following words.

examination ▪ assessment ▪ educational ▪ presence ▪ learning ▪ exercise

1 CTDUNALIOE ______________: an experience where you learn a lot

2 SSMSSETAEN ______________: a procedure to find out what a student already knows

3 RXECESIE ______________: a piece of homework to practise something

4 MAXIOTAENNI ______________: another word for a test

5 CESPERNE ______________: being there

6 GINNEARL ______________: this should take place at school and university

C Study and Teaching. Match the words with their definitions or descriptions.

1	to learn something	a	college
2	a course or programme of study	b	to study
3	an institution for higher education	c	to improve
4	to become better	d	test
5	training pupils or students	e	mistake
6	another word for error	f	teaching
7	another word for examination	g	curriculum

D Now over to You … Answer the questions using the words from page 66.

1 How do/did you like school/college? What kind of student or pupil are/were you?
2 Describe a typical day at school/college. What do/did you like? What do/did you not like?
3 What was the most important exam that you have taken? How did you manage? Did you study a lot before taking it?
4 Are you a very disciplined student? Do you have any tips?

At the Conference

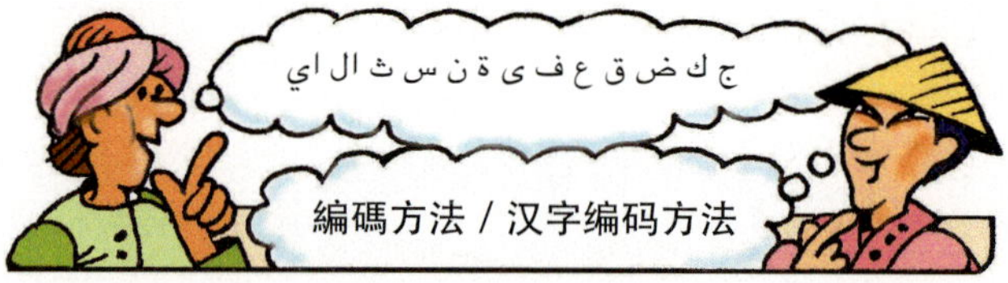

There are over 6000 different *languages* in the world.

The minister gives a *speech* at the conference today.

Mrs. Smith is *presenting* her model for the new building.

The poster *announces* "The Rolling Stones" for this Saturday.

The Language of Love

This summer Ron fell in love with a girl from Spain. The only Spanish *word* Ron knows is "hola". So he decided to take a Spanish class to be able to *talk* to her. In his class Ron learned a lot of Spanish *expressions* like "Thank you" and "Can you help me?" The most important *sentence* Ron learned – some say it is the most beautiful *sentence* in the world – was how to say "I love you!" One day Ron bought flowers and went to *express* his love to the girl. When the door opened he said, "Tee aamoo!" It was a complete surprise for the girl. Finally she said, "… *why, why* don't you just speak English to me?" After a minute of looking at each other, they both started laughing. *Of course* she speaks English!

Making a New Law

The new government *proposed* changes to the tax system. It was *proposed* that poor people should pay fewer taxes. The *proposal* about the change in the tax system was a success. All members of the parliament voted for the *proposal* to be approved. There are a lot more *details* in the new tax system. Some say all the new *details* make it harder to understand. Today's newspaper provides a lot of important *information*. It contains a special section with *information* about the new tax system. After one year the new tax system was *declared* to be a social improvement. The government *declared* it would continue to make even more changes.

To Be Precise

- Timmy is four years old and asks his mother a lot of *questions*. Many of the *questions* start with "*Why …?*" and are really hard to answer.
- To find out the meaning of a word or expression George asks his teacher for *definitions* all the time. Sometimes it is difficult for George's teacher to think of a simple and short *definition* of a word.
- Mary wanted to find out what exactly the professor meant by saying 'normal', so she asked him to *define* the term. It is especially important in science to *define* terms carefully.
- Annie made a *detailed* plan of her project before she started to work on it. She also wrote *detailed* instructions for the others in her group, so nothing could go wrong.

A Modern Talking. Complete the sentences using the following words.

of course ▪ expressed ▪ information ▪ proposed ▪ sentence ▪ speech

1 Sarah did not know which train to take. But the man behind the desk gave her all the __________ she needed.
2 "Excuse me, do you mind if I open the window?" – "No, ______________ not."
3 In parliament the minister ______________ a change of the existing law.
4 At my grandmother's 90th birthday my father got up and gave a little ______________.
5 In the interview Mr. Smith ______________ his concern about the recent political developments.
6 "Yesterday I went to …?" – "What do you mean? This is not a complete ______________!"

B Definitions. Unscramble the groups of letters to form the words described in the sentences.

1 NGLAUAEG ______________: written or spoken communication
2 PXSRSEENOSI ______________: term for a phrase or single word
3 KPAREES ______________: a person talking in front of an audience
4 TQSOEIUN ______________: a sentence or word asking for an answer or information

C Talking and Presenting. Replace the underlined words with the following words.

announced ▪ detailed ▪ meaning ▪ proposal ▪ talking ▪ why

1 Yesterday the newspaper <u>reported</u> that shops would be open until ten o'clock even on Saturdays.
2 Someone has to stop Jenny. Every time she's on the telephone she just cannot stop <u>speaking</u>.
3 The president's <u>suggestion</u> to find a peaceful solution for the conflict was rejected.
4 When I asked Susan how she always manages to get the best marks in class without ever doing her homework, she could not tell me <u>the reason</u>.
5 The teacher asked if anyone knew the <u>definition</u> of the word 'Algebra'. Of course, everyone knew it.
6 This city guide gives <u>exact</u> information about every building in town.

D Going into Detail. Match the words with their definitions or descriptions.

1	to say something officially → c	a	detail
2	something composed of letters	b	to define
3	a single fact or piece of information	c	to declare
4	to explain the meaning of a word	d	word

E Now over to You … Answer the questions using the words from page 68.

1 How many languages do you speak? Would you like to learn another language? Which one and why?
2 Are you a good speaker? Describe the characteristics of a good speaker.
3 How important do you think are exact information, detail, and definitions? In which context do you think they are more or less important?

Questions and Answers

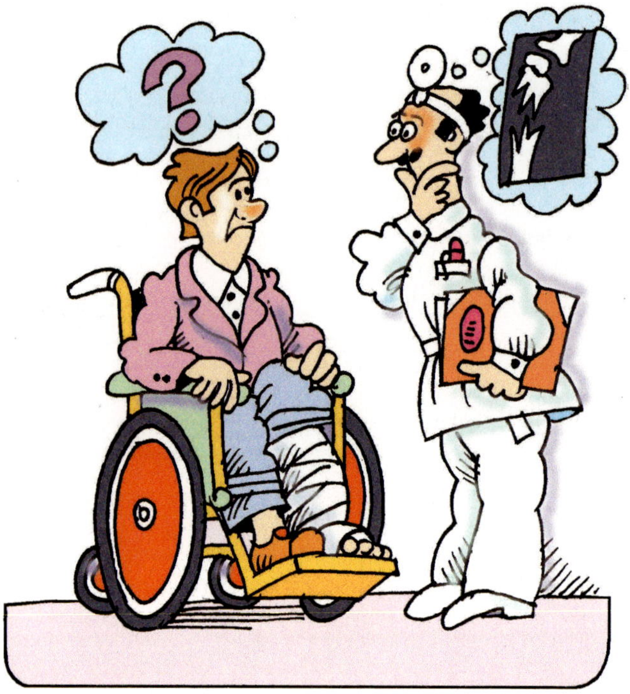

Peter *speaks* to the doctor.
The doctor *answers* his question.

When the teacher *talks* about physics,
Albert is the only one who *understands*.

A Change of Lifestyle

When Mr. Smith had a heart attack he had to be taken to the hospital. The doctor said that Mr. Smith was overweight. To lose weight, the doctor *suggested* that Mr. Smith should eat better food: *for example*; less chocolate and coffee, more bread and tea. *Understanding* the connection between being overweight and the risk of heart attack helps people change their lifestyle. In *response* to what the doctor said, Mr. Smith decided to start living healthier.
After a long *conversation* with his wife, he made an *agreement* with her that they would exercise together every day.

Bad News

Yesterday Susan received an e-mail from Tim: "I tried to call you all day but you did not *answer* your phone.
I want to *explain* to you what happened last night. The girl you saw me with .... I have to *admit* that she is my new girlfriend. I am so *sorry*! Tim."
Susan did not *understand*. Why did Tim not love her any more? Why did he not come over and *explain* to her what happened? She did not *approve* of his behaviour and she was very angry. After a week Susan *replied* to Tim's e-mail: "*Please* leave me alone!"

A Speech

Yesterday the executive at the company invited us to a nice dinner to *thank* us for our good work.
Before the dinner the executive made a speech in which he *addressed* all employees.
He said that our constant good work is the *explanation* for the company's success.
Then he said, "*Thanks* to everybody!" That night, some employees asked the executive about raising wages, but the executive did not *respond* to those questions.

A Making Networks for Language. Use words from page 70 and add more words you know.

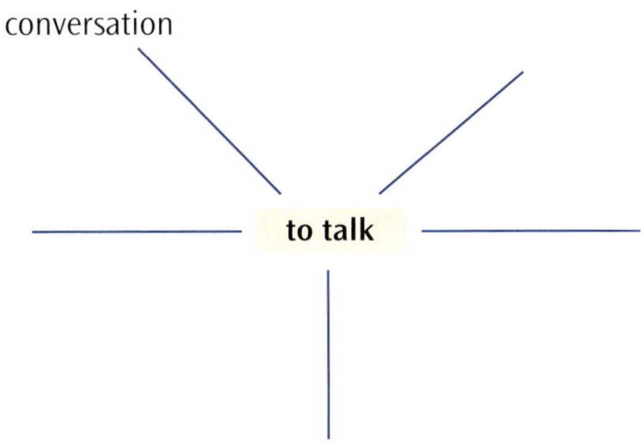

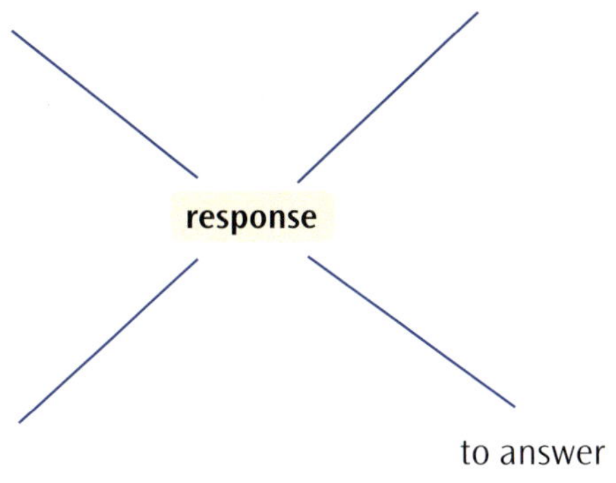

B Understanding Each Other. Complete the sentences with the following words.

answer ▪ example ▪ explanation ▪ for example ▪ please ▪ sorry ▪ talk ▪ thanks

1 Tom should really make an effort to find a new job. Instead all he does is ________________ about it.

2 I called him twice but he did not ________________ my calls.

3 “Would you ________________ help me carry these bags home?”

4 Last night three people escaped from prison. The police have no ________________ of how they managed to get out of their cells.

5 “I just wanted to say ________________ for helping me while I was sick.”

6 Annie’s cat died yesterday. All her friends feel ________________ for her.

7 John will be able to understand what you are talking about if you give him an ________________.

8 At the university you can take classes in many different subjects, ________________ in math, science, art, and history.

C For Better Understanding. Match the words with their definitions or descriptions.

1 to address	a to propose a plan or an idea to other people
2 to admit	b an arrangement between people or parties
3 agreement	c a reaction or answer to a recent event
4 response	d to agree that something is true
5 to suggest	e to give a speech to a group of people

D Now over to You … Answer the questions using the words from page 70.

1 Have you ever had an argument with someone? What happened and how did you solve the argument?
2 Do you think all children should have to learn a foreign language at school? Why or why not? Explain your answer.
3 If you have problems following a conversation, what do you do? Describe the situation.

Don't Lie!

Every time Pinocchio *lies* his nose grows longer.

There was an abandoned island which I wanted to visit. Unfortunately, *there was* a crowd of people who had the same idea.

The police make a *statement* to the press. They give a *description* of the criminal. They want the press to *note* that the criminal is a very dangerous person.

The man *denies* that he committed the crime. Nevertheless he could not *deny* the fact that they found the stolen objects in his house.

From Advice to Demand

- Sarah's parents give her *advice* all the time, such as: "It is important to learn English." One day she decided not to listen to this *advice* anymore and she began to study Japanese.
- I made the *suggestion* that my friend should study in the UK for one semester to improve his English.
- Yesterday Michael asked me if I could *recommend* a good English book. I *recommended* Melville's *Moby Dick*.
- His boss *demanded* that Ron take an English class before he went to a conference in Chicago.

Writing an Article

When you write an article, the title of your article should *refer* to the content. By *describing* what you want to say in the introduction you get the attention of your readers. You can write an article for different media; *i.e.* for a newspaper or a magazine. Instead of 'for example' you can also say *'for instance'*.
The *conclusion* is the end of a speech or a text. Usually you express your main idea again in the *conclusion*. When you want to *point* to a certain issue, you want to indicate that this issue is important. Good papers *point* to the difficulties of previous studies. When you *state* something, you express your opinion in a clear and formal way. In English papers, your own opinion should be *stated* at the beginning and explored throughout the paper. To *mention* means to say or write something. You can *mention* names of people that supported you in the beginning of a book. When John published his first article, his mother said, "I am *so* proud of you!"

Official Statements

There had been reports about a plane crash but they had not been *confirmed*, so nobody knew for sure. One day later these reports were *confirmed* by the government. The president did not want to *comment* on the speculations of the press. The next day during the press conference he officially *commented* on what had happened. The president's speech was *repeated* on TV every half hour. After two days every child was able to *repeat* the speech. First investigations were *indicating* that it was not a terrorist attack. The remaining pieces *indicated* that there was no bomb. A year later the whole *account* of the accident was finished. In the *account*, the investigators reported that the accident was caused by the pilot.

A Say What You Want to Say. Replace the underlined words with the following words.

determined ▪ i.e. ▪ indicated ▪ mention ▪ so ▪ stated ▪ statement

1. "We will have to work harder tomorrow. There is still *that* much to be done."
2. In the pub, Mr. Smith told me the story of his life, but he did not *say* that his wife left him some years ago.
3. If you are building a house you can combine different kinds of material, *for example*, wood and metal.
4. "Did you hear about the famous actor who was accused of taking drugs? Yesterday he made a *declaration* in front of the press."
5. As one of the lawyers did not appear in court, the judge *decided* that a new date for the trial would have to be set.
6. The red light in the display *showed* that the battery was empty.
7. The candidate *declared* his intention to win the elections.

B Making a Statement. Complete the sentences using the following words.

conclusion ▪ describe ▪ description ▪ lies ▪ noted ▪ points ▪ there are ▪ refers ▪ repeat

1. "Could you please ____________ your question? I did not understand."
2. You can find out easily if Tom is telling the truth. Every time he ____________ his face turns red.
3. When we met, Linda gave us a detailed ____________ of the places she had visited in China.
4. The director's speech lasted three hours. Everybody was glad when he came to the ____________.
5. "Could you please ____________ to me what your dog looks like?"
6. When Mark entered the room he ____________ that someone had left the window open.
7. John has been to nearly every place in Asia, but ____________ still some countries he has not visited yet.
8. In his book, the scientist ____________ to other publications dealing with the same subject.
9. In their report, Greenpeace ____________ to the dangers of nuclear energy.

C Descriptions. Match the words with their definitions or descriptions.

1	account	a	to say that something is not right or true
2	to recommend	b	an idea or plan for consideration
3	to confirm	c	to say very firmly that you want something
4	for instance	d	to tell someone that something is good
5	to deny	e	another expression for 'for example'
6	suggestion	f	another word for 'report'

D Now over to You … Answer the questions using the words from page 72.

1. Do you often ask for advice or give advice to family or friends?
   Describe the situation in which you last asked for or received advice.
2. What do you have to consider when you write an article or a statement in your country?
3. Do you remember some big news? Describe how it was reported on TV or on the radio.

Language Operations

to *shout*

The doctor *advises* his patient to go jogging.

Making One's Point Clear

Tim said that Friday would be a good day to get together, *implying* that he was hoping for a birthday party. His wish was so obviously *implied* that his girlfriend Linda almost started to laugh. But Tim was right: it is good to *emphasise* the things that are important to you. Because Tim had *mentioned* it, Linda was able to *remind* their friends not to forget about Tim's birthday the following week. She put great *emphasis* on the party being a surprise – she told everyone how important it was that Tim would not find out, and that they should keep it a secret. They made a lot of plans. This and that had to be prepared. Tim's friends even called the radio station and *requested* his favourite song for him. The party was a big success. When his parents called that day he gave them a full *account* of everything that his friends had done for him. In the end Tim *concluded* his way of *implying* his wish for a birthday party had been a good idea.

Opinion and Discussion

Mary would *rather* go to the swimming pool in the park than to the library. She prefers swimming to reading books. Her friend called and also suggested going to the pool. It was *indeed* a wonderful day to go swimming. Mary *therefore* packed her bag and walked to the swimming pool. *However*, after a short time at the pool she felt guilty and returned home to go to the library instead. *Thus*, she spent the afternoon in the library studying like she always does.

Making Decisions

- Something that is certain and proven is a *fact*.
  In a discussion you should use proven *facts* so nobody can prove you wrong.
- An *idea* is another word for *opinion* or view. My *idea* of a good relationship is two people who trust each other.
- If you choose between two or more things you make a *decision*. Michael's *decision* to buy the green car and not the red one was influenced by his wife.
- A way of doing something or dealing with something in a certain way is an *approach*. Peter's *approach* to involving the students in the discussion was rather new.
- When you think about your possibilities you *consider* something. He *considered* what kind of job he would like.
- To talk about something and *state* your *opinion* on it is to *discuss*.
  The parliament *discussed* the new law on immigration.
- To make a choice on something is to *decide*. Mary *decided* to join a campaign against animal testing.
- To ask for something which you have a right to is to *claim*.
  George *claimed* money from the insurance company for the damages done to his car.

A Presidential Campaign. Complete the sentences using the following words.

advised ▪ claimed ▪ concluded ▪ emphasised ▪ however ▪ informed ▪ implied ▪ reminded ▪ shouted

1 Before the presidential candidate spoke to the public, his team ______________ him on which topics to discuss and which not to discuss.
2 While he was talking to the people, he ______________ his words by raising his voice every once in a while.
3 The candidate ______________ the crowd about his plans to stop the war.
4 He ______________ the audience not to forget to vote.
5 In his speech, the candidate ______________ that he would cut taxes when elected for president.
6 He also ______________ that he would spend more money on social welfare.
7 ______________ , many candidates had made these promises before but nothing had happened.
8 Some people ______________ his name and waved flags in their hands.
9 He ______________ his talk by making a victory sign.

B Opinion and Discussion I. Match the words with their definitions or descriptions.

1	account → b	a	the action of asking for something in a polite manner
2	emphasis	b	another word for 'report' or 'statement'
3	request	c	something that is generally known to be true
4	fact	d	somebody's belief or point of view
5	idea	e	another word for 'importance' or 'priority'
6	approach	f	the act of choosing one thing over another
7	decision	g	the method or way of doing something

C Opinion and Discussion II. Replace the underlined words with the following words.

considers ▪ decides ▪ discussing ▪ indeed ▪ rather ▪ therefore ▪ thus

1 Peter is preparing himself for a discussion in class tomorrow afternoon. <u>That's why</u> he is going over his notes.
2 He <u>chooses</u> to go through the papers dealing with climate change.
3 As he is very interested in this topic he is looking forward to <u>talking about</u> it in class.
4 He <u>believes</u> it to be very important to discuss ways to reduce energy consumption.
5 This seems to be something everybody can <u>really</u> get involved in.
6 Peter would <u>prefer to</u> talk about political issues than about literature or art.
7 <u>For this reason</u> he joined the political discussion group.

D Now over to You … Answer the questions using the words from page 74.

1 Have you ever been a member of a discussion group or would you like to be in one? Do you like to discuss issues? Describe the issues you like to discuss.
2 Tell somebody about the last discussion you had.
3 Have you ever heard a good speech? What was it about and how did the speaker make it interesting?

Opinion and Discussion

to *argue*

a *debate*

Mary Gets Her Way

Mary and her new boyfriend Michael went to the theatre last week and Michael did not like the play. Now Michael *refuses* to go to the theatre again. Mary knows that Michael did not enjoy the play they saw. She *supposes* that he would like it if they saw a different play. Since it is important to Mary to share her love for theatre with her boyfriend, it *matters* a lot to her that Michael likes it, too. Therefore Mary bought tickets for "Romeo and Juliet" and *voiced* her *opinion* that Michael should go with her. When Michael heard about her plan he *rejected* the *idea* – he said he would never go again! But Mary did not give up; she called Michael five times and *insisted* on Michael going at least one more time. In the end, Mary *persuaded* Michael to go with her. Michael said yes because he *regards* the interests of his girlfriend to be important for him as well. Also he *assumed* that Mary would not stop asking him until he said yes.

Considering Something

- Jenny and Chris have an *argument* about which animal to get for their son. Jenny wants a dog and Chris wants a cat. They settled the *argument* by getting both a dog and a cat.
- In our politics class we had a big *discussion* about the next elections. When the *discussion* became a little wild, Dr. Jones interrupted it.
- When Annie said that she wanted to move to France with me, I said it would be worth a *consideration*. In the end her own *considerations* stopped her from doing it.
- I am sure it was not Peter's *intention* to hurt you when he did not invite you last Saturday. His *intention* was not to bore you because old friends from high school came by.
- It was my *assumption* that Mom and Dad would visit us this weekend. Well, I was wrong. They will come next weekend.
- I was in Berlin for only two days. At least I got an *impression* of what the city has to offer. My *impression* is that it is best to visit Berlin in summer.
- Timmy is not sure if it was a good *idea* to give his dog to Chris. He has serious *doubts* that Chris will take good care of him. When he told Linda about his *doubts*, she said that he should take his dog back.
- When making a *decision*, it is important to *consider* as many *aspects* as possible. Most things have positive and negative *aspects*.

Getting Your Way

The German football team lost the world cup. *Nevertheless*, they had the chance to win the third place the week after. *Instead* of going to school, Peter wanted to stay home and watch the football game on TV that day. Peter's brother said that the German team is not a good team and that they will lose *anyway*. His mom was against his plan. He *argued* hard, even *though* he knew he could not persuade his mom of the importance of the game. She said, "You have to go to school, *otherwise* your teacher will be angry."

A Opinion and Discussion. Replace the underlined words with the following words.

intention ▪ insisted on discussing ▪ doubt

1. Mary cared very much about the proposal. She asked to discuss it right away.
2. There is a lot of uncertainty among the people concerning their job situation.
3. It was her plan to finish work before going out to a party.

B Odd One Out. Circle the word in each group that does not belong.

1. debate – discussion – argument – impression
2. to assume – to suppose – to persuade – to regard
3. opinion – aspect – assumption – consideration

C Discussing Politics. Complete the sentences using the following words.

anyway ▪ instead ▪ voice ▪ nevertheless ▪ otherwise ▪ though

1. Mark answers, "You might be right. ______________, I think that we can't really agree on this topic, can we?"
2. He adds, "I also find that we should ______________ our concern about our educational system."
3. Peter interrupts him, "But, security is always a big issue in politics ______________, right?"
4. "I can understand your argument, I still don't agree with you, ______________," Peter remarks.
5. Mark answers, "Maybe we should talk about music ______________."
6. Peter says, "That's an idea; ______________ we will continue to discuss politics until tomorrow."

D Word Search. Find eight words from this chapter in the word search.

D	R	A	D	D	A	Y	H	T	F
C	B	P	W	E	R	X	J	F	A
A	S	P	E	C	T	C	K	V	C
O	S	R	A	I	T	V	L	J	T
P	B	O	S	S	Z	B	I	D	T
I	K	A	D	I	U	I	D	E	A
N	Z	C	F	O	I	N	O	R	T
I	G	H	G	N	O	M	U	D	F
O	F	R	J	K	A	D	B	E	R
N	I	G	D	E	B	A	T	E	N

E Now over to You … Answer the questions using the words from page 76.

1. What is your favourite topic when you have a discussion? Why?
2. When did you last have to convince someone of something? What was the issue?
   What did you and the other person say? Describe the situation.
3. Do you like people who state their opinion firmly or do you prefer a more diplomatic approach? Why?

Different Kinds of Art

Peter likes modern *art*. Today he is visiting an *exhibition* in the Louvre. The Louvre is a famous *museum* in Paris.

The *band* played great *music*. All members of the *band performed* very well.

One *film* has many *scenes*.

Music Is My Love

When John was five years old he started to play an *instrument*. His favourite *instrument* was always the guitar. When he was ten years old he started to *sing*, too. First he *sang* and played the guitar by himself, but by the age of fourteen he joined a *band*. They played *songs* by famous *bands* like The Beatles. Later John started to write his own *songs*. Three years ago his *band* played in their first *concert*. John was afraid to go on *stage* and his hands were shaking. Today he is a famous musician and plays in many *shows*.

All about Theatre, Art, and Culture

- The Globe Theatre is a famous *theatre* in London where William Shakespeare's *plays* were performed. Perhaps his most famous *play* of all is "Romeo and Juliet". Many female actors dream of playing the *role* of Juliet in that *play*. Some actors say the *role* of Hamlet is most difficult.
- The *performance* of the Irish dance group last night in Berlin was excellent.
- At the *museum* many *paintings* were *displayed* that were never shown to the public before.
- Many people who were interested in buying a *painting* by Neo Rauch, came to his *gallery* in Leipzig.
- Mr. Jones loves *art*. Since he has a lot of money he bought some *paintings* for his private *collection*. His *collection* is not very big, but there are two Picassos and one Monet in his *collection*.
- In the 1950s there were only black and white *photographs*. Later colour *photographs* were invented.
- When you learn a foreign language you should also study the foreign *culture*. You'll learn more about your own *culture*, too.
- I like all kinds of *cultural* events: *theatre*, *concerts*, and *art exhibitions*. It is sad that there is often not enough money for *cultural* activities at schools.
- Sarah went to Afghanistan to write a *report* on the *cultural* situation there.

Reading and Writing

Every child learns how to *read* when going to school. Lisa is only ten years old and really loves to *read books*. The latest *book* she read was Harry Potter. Some say Goethe is one of the most famous *writers* of all times, but I am sure among kids, J. K. Rowling is the best known *writer*. When Lisa becomes older she wants to *write* her own *books*. Someday, she hopes to become a famous *author* like J. K. Rowling.

A Art and Culture. Organise the following words into three categories based on their common meaning.

art ▪ artist ▪ author ▪ band ▪ film ▪ music ▪ to perform ▪ to read ▪ to sing ▪ theatre ▪ to write ▪ writer

B Odd One Out. Circle the word in each group that does not belong.

1 show – performance – report – exhibition
2 museum – painting – collection – scene
3 audience – stage – instrument – gallery

C Hobbies and Culture. Complete the sentences using the following words.

books ▪ cultural ▪ culture ▪ displayed ▪ concert ▪ photographs ▪ role ▪ song

1 Annie is very interested in ______________ activities.

2 She loves to read. Therefore she has hundreds of ______________ in her apartment.

3 Besides reading, she does theatre in her free time. Her last ______________ was Puck in "A Midsummer's Night Dream".

4 Her new hobby is taking ______________. She likes to take pictures of animals best.

5 When she saw a famous photographer's pictures ______________ in a gallery, she fell in love with them.

6 Her favourite ______________ right now is performed by a pop group from England.

7 Last week she went to see the band at a ______________.

8 Annie could not imagine living without ______________ in her life.

D Now over to You … Answer the questions using the words from page 78.

1 How important is culture in your life? Why?
2 Do you have a hobby like singing or acting? What is it?
3 Do you play an instrument? What is it? Why did you choose this one?
4 Do you visit museums or the theatre? Which one did you like best?
5 Do you read? What is your favourite book?
6 Do you remember a cultural activity you took part in at school? Tell us about it.
7 Did your parents encourage you to become interested in culture? How did they encourage you?
8 What is your favourite band? Why?

All on Paper

The *document* is ready to be *signed*.

Interesting News

Every morning George drinks coffee and *reads* the *newspaper*. This morning he *read* an interesting *article* in the *newspaper*. The *article* was about an *interview* with the Prime Minister. During the *interview* the journalist asked the Minister what his favourite *books* were. Of course, everyone expected Charles Dickens or Virginia Woolf's *books* to be the Minister's favourite *readings*, but the Minister answered, "Donald Duck!" He said that he likes Donald Duck's short *clauses* better than Charles Dickens difficult and long sentences. The journalist *reported* that the Minister thinks Donald Duck is *literature* just like Shakespeare is. That day at work everybody talked about what was in the *press* that morning.

About a Book

J. K. Rowling is well known for the *publication* of many *books*. Her famous *books* tell the *story* of Harry Potter. The *readers* of "Harry Potter" are not only children but also adults. Every time she finished a new volume of "Harry Potter", her readers waited excitedly for the new *book* to be *published*. The *theme* of each *book* has to do with magic in Harry Potter's life. The *message* is that love always wins. In the *introduction* of her *books*, J. K. Rowling notes people who have helped her.

Media Nouns

- When you go to university you have to *read* a lot of *texts*. Sometimes the *texts* are in a foreign language.
- If you want to find out if a *book* is good, you can read the *book's review* first. Stephen Miller's new *book* about the stars has received very good *reviews*.
- By *illustrating* you can make the content of a *book* more interesting. One way of *illustrating* is to add pictures.
- Before CDs existed, the *record* used to be the medium to listen to music. Some people still buy *records*, mainly in second hand shops.
- In *literature* exams, students are often asked to write an *interpretation* of a short *story*, play, or poem. Paul's *interpretation* of the poem was very good.
- Many *magazines publish* a *list* where the most successful *books* of the month can be found. For several months "Harry Potter" was first on the *list*.

A Reading and Writing. Correct the following sentences.

1 A story is always made up by somebody.
2 A newspaper is published only once a month.
3 An interview is another word for illustration.
4 To sign something means to fill out a form.
5 A magazine provides the daily news to the public.

B Making Mind Maps. Use the following words and add more words you know.

article ▪ chapter ▪ to illustrate ▪ review ▪ letters ▪ news ▪ to note ▪ page ▪ press ▪ publication ▪ to publish ▪ to report

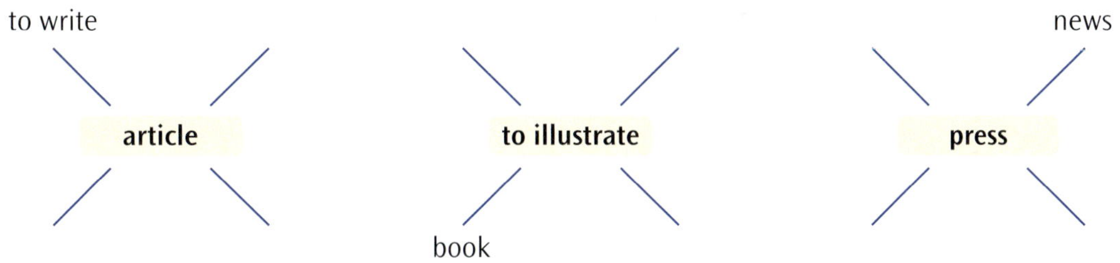

C Literature. Replace the underlined words with the following words.

document ▪ introduction ▪ message ▪ reading ▪ theme

1 Mary is very excited to go to a lecture by her favourite author, T. C. Boyle.
2 The novel's topic was a young man falling in love with an older woman.
3 In the beginning of the novel, the main characters were introduced.
4 He used a certificate to prove that he was the author of the poem.
5 The central statement of the article reflected the writer's opinion.

D Reading and Beyond. Complete the sentences using the following words.

list ▪ literature ▪ reader ▪ papers ▪ writing

1 Ron is very interested in ______________. Therefore he is always informed about the latest novels available.
2 A ______________ of the magazine complained that the articles were not very well researched.
3 Mary made a ______________ of the books she would like to get for her birthday.
4 One has to get used to Shakespeare's ______________.
5 Some daily ______________ in Germany put more emphasis on scandals than on facts.

E Now over to You … Answer the questions using the words from page 80.

1 Are you interested in literature? What is the last book you read?
2 Do you like scientific texts? What makes them different from literature?
3 Could you imagine working as a writer or journalist? What would you specialise in and why?

Games and Matches

In *football* each *team* consists of eleven players.

card

Leisure

- At the museum we saw a famous *picture* of a farmer. This *picture* was taken by a photographer 100 years ago.
- When Peter broke his leg the doctor told him to avoid certain *activities* in the future. He indicated that skiing would not be a suitable *activity*.
- Many people *prefer* reading to watching TV. Mark *prefers* reading novels to reading magazines.
- Jenny has not been on *holiday* for over two years. This year she finally decided to spend her *holiday* in Spain.
- John *plays* in the local tennis *club*. Once a year all *club* members are invited to a big party.
- Paul bought tickets for the football *match* on Sunday. His favourite *team* plays in the *match*.
- Our son loves to *play games* on the computer. My favourite *game* is basketball.
- Sarah never showed much *interest* in watching films. Reading was of much more *interest* to her.

Activities

- Susan can run very fast. In the last *race* she nearly ran twice as fast as her opponents.
- We only have three weeks left to finish our work. It will require a lot of *effort* and motivation to finish it in time. Our *efforts* will hopefully pay off in the end.
- Instead of trying one diet after another, you should really start *exercising*. It is definitely the best way to lose weight. When I want to *exercise*, I go swimming.
- Basketball *players* practise to *aim* very carefully. If you don't take enough time to *aim* at the hoop, you will miss it.
- Susan was a very active person and *used* to eat at least five meals a day. Now she only eats three times a day.
- Chris is an artist. He is *interested* in art. I am more *interested* in literature.
- Australia has one of the best cricket *teams* in the world. Last year they even won the world *championship*.
- When she was a child, Jane could *play* football all day long without noticing anything around her.
- Annie *plays* softball very well. Last week she *struck* the *ball* across the field with a strong swing of her bat. Her dad showed her how to *strike* the *ball*.

Sports and Entertainment

- Some people like to go to a *pub* to watch *sports games* on TV. Others do not like the drinking and the noisy atmosphere in a *pub* and rather watch the *games* at home.
- We will go on a *trip* to the UK next year. When I am there, I would like to visit London and Oxford.
- When you *draw*, you make a picture using a pen instead of a brush. "Dad? Can you *draw* a horse for me?"
- Last night was really nice, I *enjoyed* it a lot. I *enjoy* going to the pub with friends.
- My room in the *hotel* is rather noisy. Next time I go to Munich, I will choose a different *hotel*.
- Tim loves *sports*. He *plays* tennis and *football*. Mike does not *play sports* but watches a lot of *sports* on TV.
- Ron's *aim* for this *game* is to *play* well. Michael's *aim* is to win the *championship* this year.
- In a *league*, different *sport teams play* against each other. If we win this *game*, we are in first place in our *league*.

A Exercising. Unscramble the groups of letters to form the words described in the sentences.

1 YREPAL ________________: a person participating in a game

2 LDYAHOI ________________: period of time which you can spend visiting other countries

3 TERFOF ________________: amount of energy you need to do or achieve something

4 RSTENITE ________________: the sensation that you want to know or learn more

5 GELUAE ________________: different sport teams put together in one group

B On Holiday. Complete the sentences using the following words.

to aim ▪ championship ▪ holidays ▪ interested ▪ picture ▪ play ▪ struck ▪ used

1 The child drew a ____________ of his family.

2 Annie wrote me a letter. The cold and rainy weather is bothering her a lot. She wonders if she will ever get ____________ to the climate.

3 Paul loves sunny weather. That is why he always spends his ____________ in exotic countries.

4 It is a common belief that girls ____________ with different things than boys.

5 My father taught me how ____________ carefully before shooting.

6 Someone had ____________ the victim on the back of his head.

7 My grandfather played football in his youth. He even won the European ____________ with his team.

8 Maybe some people do not have any hobbies. But they must at least be ____________ in something.

C At the Hotel. Match the words with their definitions or descriptions.

1 card	a to like one thing better than another
2 team	b to like something while you do or experience it
3 to aim	c a group of people playing together
4 to prefer	d a note with a picture you send when you are on holiday
5 to enjoy	e something you do when you do not want to miss your target

D Odd One Out. Circle the word in each group that does not belong.

1 activity – sport – pub – to exercise
2 trip – ball – football – goal
3 game – match – interest – race

E Now over to You … Answer the questions using the words from page 82.

1 What do you prefer to do in your free time? Describe your favourite activity.
2 What sport do you like best? Do you have a favourite sports team?
3 Describe a trip you took. What did you do while you were there?

Love and Friendship

Lily and Linda are best *friends*.

Relationships

- Tim wanted his *friend* Paul to meet his sister Annie. He *introduced* them at his dinner party.
- Peter could not take his eyes off the pretty woman at the bar. So, he *approached* her and offered her something to drink.
- Mike and Mary ended their relationship a year ago. Mike moved out and hasn't been in *contact* with Mary ever since.
- Susans problems in her relationship got so bad that they even *affected* her professional life.
- She became so unhappy that she *accepted* an offer to work with another company and moved to another part of the country.
- Annie is a liberal mother. She *allows* her children a lot of things other mothers would not allow.
- George and Ron are very close and know a lot about each other. They *share* many secrets.
- Parents usually love their children very much. They are very *attached* to them.

Personal Contact

- John and Paul stopped talking years ago. They refuse to have any kind of *communication*.
- Jane and Mike have been together for ten years. They have a strong *connection*.
- Peter's mother always worries about his work. She also has some serious *concerns* about his new girlfriend.
- Ron's wife works very hard and runs the household, too. He has a lot of *respect* for her.
- After ending her relationship with Paul, Susie did not *contact* him for over two years.
- John wanted to give Mary a *present* to celebrate that they had been together for fifteen years. He decided to get her fifteen red roses and an expensive ring.
- John and Mary shouted at each other all evening. They had a terrible *row*.

Nature of Relationships

- Susan works from nine to five every weekday. She always *lets* her children watch TV until she comes home.
- Annie believes in her son's talents. That's why she *encouraged* him to take part in the competition.
- The old woman needs her children to take care of her. She *depends* on their help.
- John told Mary that he would never leave her. He *promised* to stay with her for the rest of his life.
- Annie went out with an older college student and her parents did not know. She *relied* on her brother not to tell their parents about it.
- Jane's new boyfriend *influences* her so much, I don't think she has any opinion of her own.
- Linda does not like bars. She *avoids* going to bars because they are so noisy.

A Love and Hate. Organise the following words into categories according to their meaning and add other words and expressions you know.

to attach ▪ contact ▪ communication ▪ to introduce ▪ to rely on ▪ to avoid ▪ to depend on ▪ connection ▪ concern

B Odd One Out. Circle the word in each group that does not belong.

1 concern – to approach – connection – to contact
2 to let – to avoid – to encourage – to allow
3 present – friend – respect – to depend

C Relationships Change. Complete the sentences using the following words.

attached ▪ promised ▪ affect ▪ row ▪ influenced ▪ share ▪ accept ▪ present

1 Tim and Susan were a very happy couple. They hardly ever had a ______________.

2 They were so ______________ to each other that they were hardly seen by themselves.

3 Tim gave Susan a wonderful ______________ to celebrate their first year together.

4 They used to ______________ almost everything, even their most secret thoughts.

5 When they got married, Tim ______________ Susan that they would have at least three children.

6 But he did not ______________ her wish to go back to work after the first child was born .

7 He said she was ______________ by her best friend who is a mother and has a fulltime job.

8 Now Tim has rows with his wife all the time. His problems are so bad they even ______________ his health.

D Now over to You … Answer the questions using the words from page 84.

1 What is very important in a relationship?
2 What are the things that make a good relationship work?
3 Are you married or in a steady relationship?
4 How did you get to know your partner?
5 Describe your perfect partner's looks and character.

Love and Marriage

Personal Contact

- A mother is attached to her children. She *loves* them very much.
- Tom is very important to his sister Susan. She *cares* a lot for him.
- After Paul had asked Mary ten times to become his wife, she finally agreed to *marry* him.
- When Ron told Annie that he had fallen in *love* with another woman, she started to *cry* and throw things at him.
- Jenny and Mark are having a great time together. They *match* perfectly.
- After Sarah had lied to Paul, he lost his *trust* in her and never believed her again.
- Ron and Annie broke up. Ron moved out and left Annie by herself. Now she is sad and all *alone*.
- Peter and Susan are very attracted to each other. But it is more than just a *sexual relationship*.
- Mary is tall and thin. Mark is rather short. They are a strange *pair*, but they *love* each other very much.

Social Life

- There were a lot of *people* waiting at the airport, but the police checked the passport of each individual.
- Mrs. Smith enjoys inviting her neighbours to her house. She *loves* to *meet people*.
- The tourist guide led a *group* of Japanese *people* to the Eiffel Tower. They were a *group* of about 20.
- Mike always votes for the Democratic *Party* because it's a tradition in his family.
- Mike also supports Greenpeace activities. He has been a *member* of this organisation for more than a year.
- A study shows that young *people* who belong to a religious *community* have fewer problems with drugs and violence.
- The government formed a *committee* to investigate the reasons for the plane crash.
- The killing of Martin Luther King was a sad and terrible *event* in history that no one will ever forget.
- The majority voted for the candidate from the socialist party. Over 60% of the voters *supported* him.
- In *general*, *people* tend to believe almost anything that is shown on television.
- Annie plans to *involve* as many *people* as possible for the protest march against nuclear weapons next week.
- Peter has a very demanding job. Because he works in a hospital, he has to be *available* almost all the time. That's why he never has time for anything else.

A Relationships. Correct the following sentences.

1 If you care for somebody, you don't want to help them.
2 Two people who match should not live together.
3 If you trust someone you would not tell him or her all your secrets.
4 Ron avoids being together with Mary so he must be in love with her.
5 Mary loves to meet new people, that's why she stays at home all the time.

B Personal Contacts. Unscramble the groups of letter to fill in the blanks in the sentences.

1 John loves his freedom. He has decided that he will never ______________ RYRAM.

2 Annie believes in ghosts. She does not like being ______________ ELOAN.

3 In biology class, the students learn about diseases passed on by ______________ LESXUA contact.

4 Mark is the perfect ______________ RRPTAEN. Every day he washes the dishes, cleans the house, and cooks a nice meal for his wife.

5 Paul has been married three times. This is his third ______________ EGRIRMAA.

6 Susan believes everything her husband says. She has a lot of ______________ TTSUR in him.

7 Mark is very tall, Jenny very short. They are a funny-looking ______________ RAIP.

8 You should be in ______________ VEOL with someone when you marry them.

C Definitions. Match the words with their definition or descriptions.

1 to meet	a to help and encourage somebody
2 to involve	b someone who belongs to a group or club
3 to support	c usually
4 a party	d something that has happened
5 a member	e an option
6 an event	f to include somebody in something
7 in general	g to go to see someone
8 available	h a group of people with the same political views

D Lots of People. Put the following words in order, beginning with the smallest amount of members.

group ▪ couple ▪ party ▪ committee

____

____

E Now over to You … Answer the questions using the words from page 86.

1 Do you belong to a certain group or party? If not, why not? Which one could you imagine belonging to? Why?
2 Would you like to get married one day? Why do people get married? What do you imagine a good marriage to be like?

Responsibility

Sometimes you see *poor* people in the street asking for money.

Little Timmy lost his mother in the *crowd*.

A Warm Welcome

Mary went to *visit* her friend Jenny in Japan last month. At the airport she was *welcomed* by her friend's parents. People in Japan have a long tradition of treating their guests very nicely, which is why Mary felt at home at once. When Mary's friend took her to the city center, she realised that *everyone* seemed to be rather busy. Mary's friend proposed to *lead* her to a spot from which you could see the whole city. Being a *visitor* in a foreign country, Mary learned to respect the rules of Japanese society. Mary spoke with a lot of people and asked a lot of questions. This *contributed* to her understanding of the country and its culture. As a result of her visit, Mary will always *associate* Japan with nice memories.

At the Ball

All the fans of the city football team meet regularly at the sports *club*. Last year the city team won so many matches that a lot of people *joined* the *club* – that is, they became members. The sports *club* of the city organises a big and formal party every year. Because this *ball* is a very popular event in the region, it *gathers*, or brings a lot of football fans together. The *club* only *invites* people with a *membership*, so in order to go to the *ball* you have to belong to the *club*. At the party, people have dinner and dance. The *bar* where guests can meet and drink alcohol is very popular.

Fight for Human Rights

Paul is a member of an *organisation* which fights for human rights in poor countries. Paul is the director of finances of the *organisation*. Therefore he has to bear a lot of *responsibility*. One of the goals of the *organisation* is to support the struggle for *civil* rights in South America. Paul believes that every *individual* should have equal rights and duties with no regard to social status or origin.

Many people make *contributions* to the *organisation's* cause. During the last few years, the *organisation* has established contact to other *associations* which are concerned with similar issues. From time to time Paul makes *visits* to poor countries. When he gets home, he writes reports about the actual needs and problems in these countries. Paul has learned that human rights are closely linked to a country's *leadership* or government.

A People and Responsibilities. Unscramble the groups of letters to form the words described in the sentences.

1 UTSEG ____________: someone who has come for a visit or has been invited

2 SOREPBLIYTINSI ____________________________: a duty or something you have to take care of

3 CORWD ________________: a lot of people gathered in one place

4 VIDINULAID ______________________: a single person rather than a group

5 DRASLEEPHI ______________________: the skill of governing or leading others

B Odd One Out. Circle the word in each group that does not belong.

1 to join – visitor – to gather – to invite
2 club – association – contribution – organisation
3 guest – to welcome – visit – civil

C Our Club. Complete the sentences using the following words.

contributed ▪ membership ▪ visited ▪ led ▪ associated ▪ everyone ▪ bar ▪ poor

1 Last week my uncle from Australia ____________________ me. I proposed that he come to the meeting of our club, which was to be held that evening.

2 As a ____________________ student I could not afford to take a taxi, so my rich uncle offered to pay.

3 I did not expect all our members to come to the meeting, but when we arrived ____________________ had come.

4 The meeting was held in a ____________________. We ordered some drinks before we continued with the discussion.

5 At first, we discussed if ____________________ in our club should be restricted or if everyone should be allowed to join.

6 After a long discussion which ____________________ to nothing, we decided to move on to the next point.

7 Our club has been ____________________ with other organisations which have similar causes. Not everyone was happy about that.

8 The drinks we had during the discussion ____________________ to a more comfortable atmosphere. In the end, we began telling each other stories and forgot all about our main purpose.

D Now over to You ... Answer the questions using the words from page 88.

1 Imagine you are organising a ball. How do you organise it? Who will you invite? How do you invite them? How many guests will come to the ball? Where is it going to take place?
2 If you are a member of a club or organisation, give a short description of its cause.

Political Actors

The people *demonstrated* in front of the *government* building for one week.

Politics 1

- The *government* is the authority that rules and organises a country.
- A *system* indicates the way to structure and organise things. A democracy is a *political system*.
- A *policy* is a programme or plan. The president supports a new *policy* promoting international trade.
- A *union* is a group of states joined together. The European *Union* has 27 member states.
- A *campaign* is an action often used in politics to support a political candidate winning the election.
- An *affair* is an event or occasion. The Russian president's visit was treated as a special *affair*.
- A *survey* is when a group of people are asked questions about a certain topic.
- The *current* prime minister of the UK was elected in 2007.
- *'Important'* is another word for 'relevant' or 'central'.

Politics 2

- The eagle is the *national* symbol of the Federal Republic of Germany.
- After the fall of the Wall there was a *change* in the political system in Eastern Germany.
- Journalists tend to quote people without referring to the *context*. The *background* of a person is important if you want to understand what he meant.
- When the committee arrived, many of the president's team *attended* the official meeting.
- The political party has difficulties in winning the majority. They will have a *problem* winning the election.
- Everybody was watching the outcome of the elections. It seemed like the whole country was paying *attention*.
- The whole political system broke down. The national *crisis* could not be stopped.
- The *situation* of illegal immigrants is very difficult. They hardly have any rights.
- As a politician you have to *handle* political issues with care.

Current Events

- Suddenly a journalist appeared and took pictures of the queen. He had *emerged* from behind a tree.
- Nobody had experienced something like this before. It *happened* for the first time.
- The *incident* of the minister falling off his chair during an interview is an event nobody will ever forget.
- Since a crowd was gathered, the politician took the *occasion* to talk about his opinions.
- The strike of the people working in the public transport sector was the *cause* for Paul being late.
- Unemployment and health insurance are difficult *issues* in the USA.
- After so many years, global warming is finally a *matter* everybody wants to talk about.

A Political Terms 1. Organise the following words into categories according to their meaning and add other words and expressions you know.

affair ▪ to attend ▪ to emerge ▪ government ▪ to handle ▪ to happen ▪ incident ▪ minister ▪ occasion ▪ president ▪ situation ▪ union

B Political Terms 2. Match the words with their definitions or descriptions.

1 to demonstrate → f
2 a crisis
3 a policy
4 a survey
5 a context
6 a cause
7 a change
8 a problem

a is a disaster
b is a study where people are asked questions
c is a reason
d is a transformation
e is a difficulty
f is to protest
g is a programme
h is the circumstances

C Political Affairs. Complete the sentences with the following words.

attention ▪ background ▪ campaign ▪ current ▪ important ▪ issue ▪ matter ▪ national ▪ political

1 Nobody knew about the presidential candidate's ________________ until one journalist wrote an article about him.
2 Annie is very interested in politics. She is very ________________.
3 The Green Party started a ________________ to save the earth.
4 The whole nation watched the queen's speech. She always receives a lot of ________________.
5 The outcome of the ________________ survey proved that the country was not ready to join the EU yet.
6 It was very ________________ to the citizens to meet their favourite candidate in person.
7 The ________________ president of the United States is visiting the UK.
8 The president declared the war to be an ________________ of highest priority.
9 It was only a ________________ of time until the protest would stop.

D Now over to You … Answer the questions using the words from page 90.

1 Are you interested in politics? Which national issues are you interested in? Which international issues?
2 Would you like to get involved with politics? What do you imagine life as a politician to be like?

Politics

It is the day of the *election*. Most of the people are going to *vote* for their party.

Democratic Issues

- In a democracy all men and women should be *equal*.
- In many democratic countries a new *president* is *elected* every four years.
- The *leader* of a *political* party is usually a person with a lot of influence.
- Lady Di was a member of the *royal* family of England.
- The manager is going to be away for some weeks. John will act as his *deputy* and make decisions in his place.
- The UN is an *institution* which deals with international conflicts all over the world.
- The text for the new law has been finished. Now it will have to be accepted by the *congress*.
- Germany is a *republic*. A new *government* is *elected* in a democratic *election* every four years.

International Issues

- George never showed much interest in *politics* when he was young.
  Now he is mainly interested in international issues.
- Over 190 nations are members of the UN. Among them, the USA, Russia, and
  China were some of the first nations which joined.
- The United *States* consist of 50 *states*. Alaska is the biggest of all American *states*.
- The *Ministry* of Health published a list of new health concerns. Some claim some important issues are missing.
- The candidate won with a majority of 90%. Some people said that the *votes* had not been counted correctly.
- Representatives of employers and employees met last week. It took them several *sessions* to end the strike.
- Yesterday a *cabinet* meeting was shown live on television. At one point in the discussion the *Minister* of Defence started shouting at the *Minister* of Finance.
- The *government* established a *commission* to examine the reasons for the plane crash.
  The report of the *commission* said that the weather conditions were responsible for the accident.

A Born Leader

My husband is a member of *parliament* – the group of politicians who make and change laws. – Is he a *lord*? – No, he isn't. But he hopes that the queen will grant him this title. Last week he held a speech concerning the *reforms* in the health *system*. He wants to improve the *system* by a *reform*. In every debate concerning this subject, he is the *leader*. When he was a student he became interested in the issue and took the *initiative* whenever he could. It was interesting to listen to him when he talked about the necessary changes in *legislation*. Now he works with a *commission* to change some laws to make the health *system* more effective. It is quite difficult for him to convince the members of the *conservative* party, though. This week he is invited to an *assembly* of health experts in our district where he will present his point of view.

A Living in a Democracy. Complete the sentences using the following words.

equal ▪ assembly ▪ election ▪ vote ▪ initiative ▪ international ▪ conservative ▪ elected ▪ reform

1 The situation in our schools is becoming critical. What we need is a ____________________ to improve the conditions for teachers and pupils.

2 Some men in politics would do everything to win the next ____________________.

3 It was Martin Luther King Jr.'s dream that all men should be ____________________.

4 My father is not very open to liberal influences and ideas. You could call him ____________________.

5 In a democratic country everybody can ____________________ for the candidate they want.

6 Listening to the members of the party, it is pretty clear who will be ____________________ President next week.

7 There are plans to close down the local factory. If we don't take the ____________________, we will lose our jobs.

8 Freedom of ____________________ means that you are allowed to gather without being stopped by the government or the police.

9 Jenny works for an ____________________ company whose products are being sold all over the world.

B Odd One Out. Circle the word in each group that does not belong.

1 congress – lord – parliament – cabinet
2 king – ministry – prince – queen
3 politics – state – nation – republic

C Voting. Match the words with their definitions or descriptions.

1	royal	a	a large organisation that has a particular kind of work
2	deputy	b	a formal choice for somebody or something
3	session	c	belonging to a king or queen
4	leader	d	a group of people who deal officially with a particular matter
5	legislation	e	a person who guides a group of people
6	to vote	f	someone who is in charge when the boss is gone
7	commission	g	set of laws passed by the parliament
8	institution	h	a formal meeting

D Now over to You … Answer the questions using the words from page 92.

1 Name some countries which still have a queen or king.
2 What are reasons for or against this form of government?
3 Are you interested in politics? What issues are you interested in?
4 Are you intested in elections? Why is it important to vote in a democracy?

War and Peace

In the sixties, hippies fought for global *peace*.

The *United* Nations have their main building in New York.

A History of War

If you look at the history of the earth you might think we cannot exist without *wars*. A lot of men and women always get *killed* in *wars* – *soldiers* as well as civilians. But it is not a thing of the past: there are still *wars* today. Nearly every country in the world has an *army* with *soldiers*. They learn how to use *weapons*; for example, how to *shoot* with a *gun*. They also learn about *strategies* in *war* – how to form a plan and carry it out. Sometimes a *war* ends with a *treaty* of *peace* but the situation in Israel and Palestine shows that even several *treaties* do not help to stop the *conflict*.

National and International Issues

- Nearly all houses in the village were *destroyed* after the enemy *soldiers* attacked.
- If a country starts a nuclear *weapons* programme it is a serious *threat* for the world.
- With the *Treaty* of Paris the United States finally became *independent* in 1783.
- Freedom of speech is one of the most essential values of a *democratic* system.
- The workers were on *strike* for *several* days and did not want to leave the factory.
  The police had to use *force* to get them out.
- Mary has taken several self-*defence* classes to protect herself in case she is attacked.
- Her father adopted a rather *liberal* approach when he raised his daughter.
- In response to the danger of a civil *war*, the UN sent *troops* to keep order and *peace*.
- Tom and his father have been arguing all week. It is difficult to say when their *conflict* started.
- *Leading* politicians will take part in the *peace* talks, so we hope they will be successful.

Then and Today

- The French *revolution* gave birth to a democratic system in Europe.
  In the course of this *revolution* most members of the royal family were killed.
- The *candidate* of the conservative party won the election this year.
- The *Battle* of Trafalgar ended in a great victory for the British Empire.
  It is considered to be the greatest *battle* on sea in that period.
- 'Collateral damage' is a *military* term, explaining why people are killed in the course of a *military* operation.
- The opposition party will need a *majority* of over 50% to establish a working government.
- Greenpeace sent a *representative* to talk with the head of the environmental protection department.
  They discussed the problem and finally came up with a solution.
- Germany has *regulations* for the sale of weapons. Without these *regulations* everyone could easily get access to dangerous *guns*.

A Join the Army. Replace the underlined words with the following similar words.

force ▪ threat ▪ leading ▪ regulations ▪ liberal ▪ gun ▪ strategy ▪ representative ▪ shoot

1 Our old neighbour used to fire at birds in order to protect the fruit on his trees.
2 During the Cold War, the possibility of a nuclear war was a danger which concerned everyone.
3 The government has developed a new plan to reduce taxes in the country.
4 You can always achieve much more by finding the right words instead of using violence.
5 An illness prevented the president from taking part in the conference, so he sent a deputy in his place.
6 Nobody understood the new tax limitations which were introduced by the government.
7 Jenny is member of a human rights organisation. She wants everyone to have a more open attitude towards people from other countries.
8 Peter loves to watch wild west movies. Unfortunately he cannot afford to buy a horse and a weapon, so he just keeps on watching his films.
9 Because he received the best results on the examination, Chris could work wherever he wanted to.

B First Strike. Complete the sentences using the following words.

independent ▪ weapon ▪ revolution ▪ majority ▪ defence ▪ candidates ▪ united ▪ army

1 England is often referred to as the "______________ Kingdom".
2 The nuclear bomb is a ______________ which was first used during the Second World War .
3 At the age of 18, Mark had to join the ______________ and learn how to use a gun.
4 Our troops attacked with every man but we just could not break through the enemy's ______________.
5 In Europe the ______________ of people prefer to go by car rather than by bike.
6 The Bastille was attacked and destroyed at the start of the French ______________.
7 Most African countries had to fight colonial wars before they finally became ______________.
8 There were over a hundred ______________ for the job, but Lisa had the luck to be chosen.

C Odd One Out. Circle the word in each group that does not belong.

1 war – conflict – peace – battle
2 to kill – to attack – strike – to destroy
3 troops – soldier – military – treaty

D Now over to You … Answer the questions using the words from page 94.

1 War is often seen as the easiest solution to a conflict between two parties. What alternative ways of ending a conflict can you think of?
2 What do you think of anti-war movies? Discuss the logic of having or not having this kind of film.
3 Have you ever talked with anyone who has been in a war? What did she or he tell you?
4 Do you think self-defence classes are useful?

Financial Market

Linda studied *finance* at the university. She wanted a career that dealt with the management of money. She found a job on Wall Street as a trader on the stock *market*. This is no ordinary *market* where people buy and sell fruit. Instead, Linda buys and sells *shares*. People buy these little parts of companies hoping to make an *investment*. They hope that the money they put in the company by buying *shares* will be more when they sell the *shares*. They hope the *rate* or worth of the *shares* goes up so that they will make money. Linda loves that her job deals with *financial* matters.

Heavy Metal and Things

- George has a job in the automobile *works*. Thousands of cars are made there every day.
- To show his love, John gave Susie a ring made out of *gold*. It was very expensive.
- Many people argue about *nuclear* power. Some say it is very clean and good for the environment and others say it is dangerous.
- Michael's car was out of *gas*. He had to walk because he forgot to fill it at the last stop.
- Bills are made from paper and coins are made from *metal*.
- Things like *gas* or paint are no longer made with *lead*, because it is bad for the environment.
- The old trains used *coal* as a power source. It was burned to make a hot fire in the train's engine.
- Many scientists say that there is only enough *oil* for about 100 years. After it is all gone we will have to find another source of power for our cars.
- Because nobody was buying their products, the company closed their *plant*.

A Country's Needs

- Chris had a job in the city's *industrial* area. Much business was conducted in this area.
- Many countries are trying to use more solar *energy*.
- The device was made from many different *materials*. It had over 50 different component parts.
- The factory where Tim worked wanted to increase *production*. They wanted to make more of their product so that they could make more money.
- Because they were not selling enough cars, the company offered a *reduction* in price. They hope to sell more cars with a lower price.
- Every year, the members of the company's board meet to discuss the *economic* plan for the year. They discuss the business and how they will manage the company's money.

Government Help

The government decided it needed to help with the *development* of the country. They wanted to help the country grow. They decided that the best way to do this would be to help improve the country's *industry*. By helping to make the country's professional activity better, the country would have more jobs for its people. Their first act was to find money in their yearly *budget* for their new task. This money helped the *output* of the factories and businesses in the country. Because they produced more, they were able to sell more. All this helped improve the country's *economy*. More people had jobs and had money to spend.

A Economy Matters. Complete the sentences using the following words.

oil ▪ development ▪ finance ▪ gold ▪ investment ▪ shares ▪ output ▪ economic ▪ market

1 The factory increased its ________________ every year. It made more of its product.
2 Most countries in the world have a stock ________________. People buy and sell shares there.
3 Many people who work at banks study ________________. It is helpful to them to know about the management of money.
4 Many different things are made out of ________________, including plastics and gas.
5 Mark noticed the ________________ of the area when he made his visit. There was much growth and progress.
6 Mary had to give up her car for ________________ reasons. She could no longer afford it.
7 Peter bought some shares of a big company, hoping to make an ________________.
8 Wedding rings are usually made out of ________________.
9 Many people on Wall Street work as traders on the stock market and buy and sell ________________.

B Odd One Out. Circle the word in each group that does not belong.

1 metal – gold – lead – gas
2 plant – farm – works – industrial
3 rate – nuclear – coal – energy

C Definitions. Match the words with their definitions or descriptions.

1 share → d	a putting money into something hoping to gain more
2 industry	b dealing with money
3 material	c making things
4 reduction	d a part of a company
5 production	e sum, amount to spend
6 investment	f general business activity
7 budget	g a lessening, decrease
8 financial	h management of resources in a country
9 economy	i component, element, part

D Now over to You … Answer the questions using the words from page 96.

1 Do you or anyone you know have financial investments? Can you describe them?
2 Do you have any type of industry in your area? What kind of industry? What does it produce?
3 What kind of energy is produced in your area? Is it clean energy or bad for the environment?
4 What do you know about the stock market? Did you ever buy shares of a company?
5 What do you think about nuclear power?
6 How is the economy in your country?

Chris's Car

Last Saturday, Chris saw someone take his car. He could not believe someone would commit a *crime* like this in the open. He called the *police* to come to the scene and help him. The *police* looked for *evidence*, but the man did not leave anything behind to help the *police* find him. Luckily, the *police* found a woman who could identify the man who took the car. With the woman's help, the *police* were able to *catch* the man and get Chris's car back. At first, the man tried to run away, but the *police* gave him an *order* to stop. He followed their request. The *police* were able to *charge* the man with the crime of stealing.

Rules and Regulations

- John made a *claim* that his food was too cold. The restaurant gave him a new meal.
- The people in the city made an *appeal* to the government for money for the school.
- The city *code* stated that loud parties after 12pm on weekdays were not allowed. The city rules allowed loud parties only on the weekend.
- Annie thought it was not *just* that she had to stay inside and clean her room.
- Michael's work injury *entitles* him to money from his workplace. He is also able to get money for his medical bills.
- The man was faced with a *charge* of taking something that did not belong to him.

Law and Order

- Everyone should have the *right* to be free. They should also be able to say what they want.
- Walking in public without a shirt is *legal* in many countries, but in some it is not allowed.
- When George bought his new car he signed a *contract*. The formal agreement said that he would pay every month.
- An important part of a free society is *justice*. All people should be treated fairly.
- The congressman started a new *bill* in congress. This proposal was to change a *law*.
- The child was caught in the *act* of drawing on the wall.
- It is not good when people do not follow the rules and break the *law*.

A Day in Court

Lisa had to go to *court*. She had never been in the place where all the *laws* are decided. She wanted to visit a friend, who was a *solicitor*. He helped people with legal matters and defended them in a *trial*. Today, Lisa's friend was working on a *trial* to determine if a person did or did not steal a car. The *police* said that this person, the *defendant*, did steal the car, and they were trying to *prove* it. Lisa's friend was trying to establish and show that the *defendant* did not take the car. The *judge* had to decide whose *evidence* was better and decide who was right. The *judge* heard both sides in this *legal* matter. This *case* was hard for her to decide. In the end she made her *judgement*. She decided that the *defendant* commited the crime and that he should go to *prison*. This *settlement* meant he would have to stay in *prison* for 5 years. Lisa thought it was all very interesting. She decided she wanted to become a *solicitor*, too.

A Law and Order. Match the words with their definitions or descriptions.

1	law	a	agreement, decision
2	evidence	b	something that is done
3	case	c	fairness, equality
4	justice	d	to give a right, to allow
5	to entitle	e	a rule or a set of rules
6	order	f	something used to confirm or prove something else
7	act	g	a command, request
8	settlement	h	a formal product of a legal body
9	bill	i	a legal event or proceeding

B Crime and Punishment. Complete the sentences using the following words.

appeal ▪ prove ▪ code ▪ judge ▪ charge ▪ police ▪ prison ▪ catch ▪ claim

1 The city ______________ is a collection of the rules of the city.

2 The ______________ are responsible for finding and stopping criminals.

3 The man made a ______________ that a man took his money. This was not true; he lost his money in the casino.

4 The police were happy to ______________ the criminal before he was out of the city.

5 The woman made an ______________ for help. Her request was not heard.

6 The solicitor could not ______________ that the man did not take the car.

7 The police were able to ______________ the criminal with murder.

8 The ______________ had too many criminals inside. They had to build additional buildings so that there was more room.

9 A ______________ has to decide who is right.

C Odd One Out. Circle the word in each group that does not belong.

1 judge – solicitor – defendant – bill
2 court – contract – trial – judgement
3 legal – crime – just – right

D Now over to You … Answer the questions using the words from page 98.

1 In Kansas, it is against the law to catch a fish with only your hands.
Are there any strange laws where you live?
2 Describe the legal process where you live. What happens when someone commits a crime?
What happens after the police find criminals?
3 Do you think all laws should be followed at all times? Why?

Mark's Summer Adventure

On his summer holiday Mark had nothing to do. All of the other *local* children were gone and he had nobody to play with. He did not want to go to the *library* and read a book. Even if he wanted to, they had a *policy* to not allow children. There was a *social* club in the city where he could play games, but he didn't know any of the other children. There was a swimming pool in his area but it was not *public*. It was for members only. It seemed to Mark that his area did not *offer* anything for children to do.

City Services

- A *service*, such as gas, electricity, or public transportation, is usually provided by a city for its people.
- Many people do not like to pay a *tax*. They get less money from their job and they don't like what the government does with the money.
- The *official* in the employment office gave me a form and told me to sit down.
- The *agency* in charge of water was in a large building in the centre of town.
- The letter with my power bill came in the *post* every month.
- The woman at the store didn't have the *authority* to give me my money back. Only her boss could do that.
- The central *fund* for parks had enough money to offer two new jobs. Last year there was not enough money in the *fund*.
- The university was able to give *support* to more students this year. This help came in the form of extra money.
- The fire department can only *serve* those who live inside the city. They cannot do anything for people outside the city.

Sarah's New Home

Sarah is having a difficult time finding a place to live. *Housing* is very expensive in her city and she does not have very much money. Sarah is *elderly*. Like many other old people, her *pension*, which she gets from the government, is not very much money. She has heard about a government *administration* that helps people like her find homes. This government office can *grant* money to the *elderly* to help them buy a home. Sarah thinks she will try to get this financial *aid*. With the money she can finally make an *offer* on a nice house in her area.

Michael's Visit to the Hospital

Michael was sick and he needed to go to the *hospital* so he could get better. He was happy that he had health *insurance* so that he could pay for his treatment. There was only one *hospital* for the *public* of the city where Michael lived, so he had to go there. The *council* for health was in charge of the *hospital*, so Michael knew he would get good treatment. People always said that this government office did good work. Michael took his *official* documents with him. He wanted to make sure he had the right papers when he left the house. The documents would *enable* him to get the treatment he needed.

A Services. Unscramble the groups of letters to fill in the blanks in the sentences.

1 The ________________ CPBLUI theatre was open to everyone in town.

2 After Tim drove his car into a tree he was glad he had ________________ CANISAUREN to pay for the damages.

3 It was easy to find ________________ GIOUHSN in Chicago. There are many places to live.

4 The Environmental Protection ________________ YNAGCE is a government office in charge of the environment.

5 After he left his job with the factory, Ron was given a ________________ NSPEINO. He hoped it would be enough money for him and his wife.

6 In order for the marriage documents to be ________________ FCIOLAFI the man and the woman and the priest had to sign them.

7 John's boss gave him the ________________ YHOIUATTR to order office products when he was away.

8 My new car will ________________ BEEALN me to drive to work every day. It will also allow me to drive on holiday.

9 The restaurant had a no pets ________________ CPOYIL. Dogs and cats had to stay outside.

B Odd One Out. Circle the word in each group that does not belong.

1 tax – fund – grant – elderly
2 hospital – library – social – post
3 official – administration – council – support

C In the City. Replace the underlined words with the following words.

serve ▪ service ▪ aid ▪ offer ▪ local ▪ public

1 The city government gave financial <u>help</u> to the homeless.
2 The woman was given a(n) <u>proposal</u> of 250,000 for her home.
3 The <u>nearby</u> community school gave Spanish classes every Thursday.
4 The public <u>office</u> that cost the most to run was the electric agency.
5 The motto of the police department is "To <u>perform duties</u> and protect."
6 The <u>community</u> did not like the government of their city.

D Now over to You … Answer the questions using the words from page 100.

1 What kind of services does your city provide?
2 Does the city offer much to do in your area?
3 Are there any agencies that help poor or old people in your city? Any national agencies?
4 Does everybody in your country have health insurance?

Youth Culture

In every *society* in the world, there are young people and old people. Many young people feel that their parents and older people *control* their lives. They feel like their parents always tell them what to do and where to go. As a result, many young people turn away from a *traditional* way of life. They dress and act differently from their parents and grandparents. Because of their way of life, they face much *criticism* from the older generation. Many older people say that young people *act* childish. They think their behaviour is poor. Young people are often the ones who most want to *change* the world. They think things could be better if they were different. Young people like to *choose* more young and liberal political candidates. The young people will one day be the old people of the *population*. They will then have a young generation that thinks the same things about them.

Mr. Jones Goes to Congress

The people made a *choice*. They elected Mr. Jones to *represent* them in Congress. Mr. Jones wants to make an *impact* on the way things are. He sees his job as an *opportunity* to make a change in society. He would like to be able to *head* a committee for environmental concerns. He thinks that if he can lead this committee he can help bring about *progress* and change. He will have to work with others and follow the rules and *procedures* of Congress. Only in this way, can he *complete* his goal of making a change.

A Day in Court

Jane has to *settle* a small problem. Her neighbour thinks that Jane's parties are too loud. The *standard* way to deal with this is for the two neighbours to try to agree among themselves. Jane's neighbour does not prefer the normal way, and wants to start a *process* against Jane at the local court. Jane has the opportunity to ask for *representation* in this *process*. Jane decides against the *option* to have a solicitor help her. The judge tells her that the *rule* is in favour of her neighbour. He says, however, that it is not a large offence and she can go under one *provision*. In the future, she must keep *control* of her parties, so that there is not too much noise.

A Good Park

- All people in a *free* land, no matter what colour or class, should be able to live and act, as they want to.
- Many people have the goal of helping the poor. For this *purpose*, they give money and their free time.
- The John D. Rockefeller *Foundation* is an institution, which helps support education in the world. There are many other foundations that also do good work.
- A *board* is in charge of a *foundation*. They decide who gets the *foundation's* money.
- National parks are all for public *use*. Nobody can own the land; it belongs to everyone.
- The president can *establish* new national parks. The first national park was created in 1872.
- Governments *form* national parks for many different reasons. Many are created to help the environment.
- A *tradition* of many Americans is to visit a national park in their summer holiday.

A Definitions. Match the words with their definitions or descriptions.

1	population	a	to make something different
2	to change	b	to make a choice
3	opportunity	c	the total number of people in a land
4	standard	d	a continuing pattern of beliefs or practices
5	foundation	e	a chance to achieve a goal
6	criticism	f	a negative comment or judgement
7	to choose	g	an institution that helps others
8	tradition	h	something normal or usual

B Fill in the Blanks. Complete the sentences using the following words.

progress ▪ choice ▪ traditional ▪ society ▪ form ▪ process ▪ option ▪ control ▪ complete

1 John wants to finish his project. In order to ______________ it on time he needs help.

2 The founders of the United States wanted to ______________ a democracy.

3 Jane lives in a very ______________ family. She dresses and acts the way her parents like her to.

4 In a free ______________ there are no slaves. People can think and act like they want to.

5 The judge ended the ______________ and sent the criminal to jail.

6 Mr. Smith made ______________ with his Russian. Everyone said he was better.

7 There were so many good things on the menu; it was hard for Susie to make a ______________

8 The newspapers reported that the dictator gained ______________ of the newspapers and radio.

9 George had the ______________ to either pay his taxes or go to jail.

C Synonyms. Replace the underlined words with the following words.

control ▪ act ▪ head ▪ represent ▪ procedure ▪ provision ▪ purpose ▪ establish

1 The president wants to <u>create</u> a national park in the city where he was born.
2 The <u>leadership</u> of the company voted to give themselves more money.
3 Johns <u>goal</u> in life was to become a policeman.
4 The Member of Parliament was proud to <u>speak for</u> the people of his home county.
5 There is a certain <u>method</u> you need to follow to get a bank loan.
6 To <u>lead</u> a large corporation takes a lot of education and experience.
7 The mother told her daughter to <u>be</u> like a good girl and to stop crying.
8 One <u>condition</u> for renting a car is to be 25 years old.

D Now over to You … Answer the questions using the words from page 102.

1 What are some traditions where you come from? Did you follow them when you were younger?
2 What are some things that young people do that are different from the older generations?
3 What were some of your goals when you were younger? Have they changed as you have got older?

The News Reporter

Mark works as a reporter. He doesn't work for a newspaper, you see him on *television*. Every day, he goes into a *studio* where he reports the news on camera. He doesn't report live. The cameras make a *video* of him. The *video* is played the next day on the news *programme*. Every day, Susie turns on her *TV* to watch Mark's news *programme* on *channel* 4. She doesn't watch *channel* 4 at any other time of the day.

Computer Lab

- A *computer* is an essential part of our daily life.
- A *computer* would be almost useless without *software*. I can't imagine not being able to play games, type papers, or edit photos.
- Fax machines and other *devices* can be useful attachments for a *computer*.
- Some people like to read the *technical* instructions before they use a *computer*.
- The *user* can operate a *computer* in many ways.
- Much *computer* software is *automatic*. For example, the operating system starts up without the user doing anything.
- *Computer* scientists developed a new *computer technique* that helps do stock market calculations faster.

Making Music

Annie wants to become a big pop star. She wants a famous producer to *record* her singing in a big studio. She wants to hear her songs played on the *radio* and see herself on *television*. She wants to go into a store and see people buying her music on tape or compact *disc*. Unfortunately, Annie is a very bad singer, and she doesn't know any producers. A good producer could help Annie by using *technology*. He could use a *machine* to change the sound of her voice.

Ron's Business Trip

As part of his job, Ron must often travel to different parts of the world. In some places where Ron does business it is hard to find a *telephone*. Therefore, Ron always takes his mobile *phone* with him. One time Ron was expecting a very important *call* from his boss. He waited, but he never got the *call*. His *phone* did not even *ring*. He realized that he had no reception. He was away from his *network*.

A Odd One Out. Circle the word in each group that does not belong.

1 programme – TV – channel – user
2 call – telephone – record – network
3 computer – radio – software – user

B Audio and Video. Match the words with their definitions or descriptions.

1 television → g
2 device
3 phone
4 disc
5 technology
6 video
7 ring
8 automatic

a electronic or digital products as a group
b an electronic or mechanical machine
c an object used for audio recordings
d a visual recording
e the noise a telephone makes
f being controlled or operated independently
g a visual medium
h an object used to talk with others over long distances

C Specialised Work. Replace the underlined words with the following words.

technique ▪ machine ▪ studio ▪ technical

1 Scientists developed a <u>method</u> for computers to make mathematical calculations more efficiently.
2 The band had to book the <u>recording room</u> for three weeks to finish recording their CD.
3 A(n) <u>apparatus</u> is made up of moving parts and performs some kind of work.
4 The instructions for the fax machine were very <u>specialized</u>.

D Word Scramble. Find twelve words from this chapter in the word search.

M	N	B	V	R	E	C	O	R	D	C	X	Y	A
E	N	D	F	G	H	J	K	L	P	O	I	U	S
D	E	R	T	P	R	O	G	R	A	M	M	E	Z
C	T	T	R	E	W	Q	A	Y	W	S	X	E	S
F	W	D	C	O	M	P	U	T	E	R	U	D	O
T	O	J	A	O	W	R	J	T	I	H	O	C	F
G	R	F	L	F	F	K	D	T	S	K	D	T	T
B	K	J	L	C	G	M	E	F	T	J	E	G	W
H	U	B	E	M	P	H	O	N	E	G	V	B	A
U	J	R	R	E	B	V	C	X	S	D	I	Z	R
S	K	A	T	U	R	E	H	F	Z	U	C	H	E
E	M	D	Z	U	M	A	C	H	I	N	E	N	T
R	J	I	O	K	M	I	J	N	U	H	B	N	G
L	D	O	D	T	E	L	E	P	H	O	N	E	F

E Now over to You … Answer the questions using the words from page 104.

Give some examples of technology in the workplace and in the home. Which of these devices has changed the way we live the most? What are some benefits that technology provides? What are some negative aspects of technology?

The Fire

John came home to see that there was a *fire* in his building. The *fire* was bright yellow and red and very hot. John was afraid that the *fire* would *burn* his books, bed, and all his things. He was also afraid that the other people in the building would be *burned*. Everyone and everything in the building was in great *danger*. Everyone and everything could be destroyed. He knew that he needed to *protect* the other people in the building from the *fire*. He first went to Mrs. Jones' flat to *warn* her that the building was on *fire* and that she should go outside. He then went to Mr. Smith's flat and helped him *escape* the building. When Mr. Smith was outside and safe, he went back inside to *save* Mr. Smith's dog and cat. After the *fire*, the building had much *damage*, and was nearly completely destroyed, but all of the animals and people were safe. John was a hero because he was able to *protect* everyone in the building.

Danger

- Some doctors *commit* errors in their work. The mistakes are done because they are tired.
- The older people in the community thought it was an *offence* to talk in church.
- After the football match there was much *violence*. There were many fights, and many fans broke windows and turned over cars.
- One goal of the United Nations is to *prevent* war around the world.
- When Jenny's boat turned over, she realized she was in *trouble* and could die in the water.
- The government will hold a bank *enquiry*. They will ask questions and try to find out why the bank lost so much money.

Safety

- The mother wanted to *ensure* that her baby would sleep well during the night. In order to make sure of it, she gave the baby some warm milk.
- *Security* is very important for the Olympic Games. The host country wants to make sure that everyone is safe.
- The mother told her son to be *careful* crossing the street. She wanted him to look both ways and make sure there were no cars coming.
- The Royal Society for the *Protection* of Birds is an organisation that tries to make sure that nothing bad happens to birds.
- The passengers in the aircraft were told to *secure* their bags so that they did not move around during the flight.
- The *police* are responsible for public *safety*. They make sure that the people in the city are safe.

News Flash

Yesterday a *murder* took place in the southern district of the city. The *victim* was a nineteen-year-old male. The *attack* took place somewhere between midnight and 1 am. *Police* say the murderer used the dark to *hide* so that no one could see him. Because he could not be seen, it was easier for the murderer to surprise and to *attack* the victim. *Police* arrived on the scene at about 6 am to *investigate* the scene and look for *evidence*. The *police* conducted a *search* of the area, but no *evidence* was found. The murderer is considered very *dangerous*, a threat to you and your family. If you know anything that can help the *police* in their *investigation* into this matter, please call the local *police* department.

A Keeping It Safe. Unscramble the groups of letters to fill in the blanks in the sentences.

1 The people in the city were in ______________ GRDENA from the heat wave. They could die because of the record temperatures.

2 To try to keep warm in the forest, the family built a ______________ IEFR. It kept them all warm.

3 Parliament held an ______________ YEQURIN against one of its members. They asked him questions about his actions, to make sure they were all legal.

4 The city police conducted an ____________________ TNIOVGINSETAI into who killed the young woman.

5 The boy was very ______________ FLCRAUE with his toys. He made sure that nothing bad could happen to them.

6 The rock band had extra ______________ YCSUTREI for their concert. They wanted to be safe from the audience.

7 The army led a three-day ______________ CKTATA on the small city. Much of the city was destroyed.

B Dangerous World. Match the words with their definitions or descriptions.

1	protect → c	a	something bad, a crime
2	murder	b	to do a crime or something wrong
3	search	c	to keep safe from harm, danger, injury
4	burn	d	to damage by fire
5	offence	e	the crime of killing
6	escape	f	to look for something, try to find
7	commit	g	to get away from

C Helping Out. Replace the underlined words with the following words.

warn ▪ investigate ▪ ensure ▪ protection ▪ attack ▪ secure ▪ victim

1 The man tried to <u>use violent force on</u> the old woman. The police came before he could injure her.
2 The mother wanted to <u>make sure</u> that her children were in good health. She always gave them healthy foods.
3 One job of the police is to <u>examine</u> a crime and look for evidence to find out who did it.
4 The train accident had only one <u>hurt or injured person</u>.
5 The president needed more <u>defence</u> when he travelled around the world. Many people wanted to kill him.
6 The woman tried to <u>tell about danger</u> the boy on the bicycle about the oncoming car. The boy did not listen and was injured when the car hit him.
7 When going on holiday, the family had to <u>attach</u> the bags to the top of the car. They had to make sure that the bags didn't move or fly off the car.

D Now over to You … Answer the questions using the words from page 106.

1 What kinds of news reports do you see on television? What kinds of things do they describe?
2 Have you ever done anything that was not safe? What was it? Describe it.

Hot Spots

Mr. Smith is taking a walk *outside* with his dog. The cat has to stay *inside* the house.

The cat is sitting on *top* of a wall. The man is standing *below*.

External Factor

Tom is the owner of a rather big company. He needs to visit the *location* for his new office building. He has already chosen a *sector* of the city in which the office building should be. This *area* is located close to the *centre* of the city. There is not much *space* left for new buildings. The only available property in this *sector* is located next to a *broad* street. *Around* this property is the commercial *centre* of the city. The whole *area* is filled with shops, stores and office buildings. On each *side* of the property there are big signs which read "For Sale". Due to *external* factors, like bad weather, they have not started building yet. Therefore Tom has *extended* the time for finishing the building for another six months.

Lovely Locations

Timmy's friend Peter could not join the family on their trip this weekend. There was no *space* left in the car. This time they will spend their weekend at a beautiful *place* on the coast. It is a small village called "Heacham". Their hotel is located on a beautiful *site*. There are lots of old trees and it is close to the beach.
In the morning Timmy and his parents go to the beach. On the *surface* of the sea they can see little waves. Timmy cannot swim yet. Therefore he must stay away from the *area* where the water is getting *deep*. His parents have *placed* their things close to the shore. Thus they can always see what Timmy is doing. From time to time they can see birds *above* their heads. Timmy tries to swim *under* water, but he realises that it is quite hard. Before Timmy and his parents return to the hotel they can see the sun going down in *front* of them.

Central – At the Edge

- The police caught the man who committed the crime. He was put in a *cell* so that he cannot escape.
- I found my keys. They were at the *bottom* of my bag.
- The hotel I am looking for is in *central* London. It's only a five minute walk to Buckingham Palace.
- We can go to the park and play football. I know a nice *spot* where there are few people.
- I think I'm near the museum but I don't know my *position* for sure.
- There was a fire in the house, but it only destroyed the *front* of the building. The back is intact.
- Because of the war, everybody concentrates on *external* matters. Nobody pays attention to *internal* affairs.
- I have to climb stairs a lot because I live in the *upper* part of the building.
- There are new trees at the southern *edge* of my garden. The old ones have been cut down.

A Moving. Replace the underlined words with the following words.

inside ▪ broad ▪ placing ▪ area ▪ set ▪ extended ▪ central ▪ cell ▪ space

1 Susan has moved to a new apartment which provides enough room for all of her things.
2 Her last apartment was so small that Susan's friends often compared it with a prison.
3 The doors of her new apartment are so wide that two people can enter it at the same time.
4 The former owner of the apartment has expanded it by removing some useless walls.
5 When Susan saw the interior of the apartment for the first time she knew at once that she wanted to move in.
6 Besides its many advantages, it is located in a middle part of town.
7 When she moved in, Susan had already bought a new collection of curtains for her windows.
8 The next two weeks, Susan was busy putting her possessions back in cupboards and drawers.
9 Susan was not familiar with the quarter she had moved into. So she went out to find some shops.

B Berlin. Complete the sentences using the following words.

site ▪ sector ▪ around ▪ surface ▪ below ▪ front ▪ under ▪ bottom ▪ deep

1 During World War II, Berlin was ______________ attack. Due to these attacks the major part of the city was destroyed.
2 After the war, Berlin was divided into a Russian and an American ______________.
3 The city's ______________ is beautiful. It is surrounded by large forests and lakes.
4 Some of these lakes are really ______________. They are dangerous for people who cannot swim.
5 Last year some gold was discovered at the ______________ of one of those lakes.
6 A major road which is called the "Berliner Ring" leads cars ______________ the city.
7 The highest building of the city is the so-called "Fernsehturm". You can go to the top and enjoy a great view over the city ______________.
8 In ______________ of the building you will see the red town hall which was built in the 18th century.
9 Under the ______________ of Berlin, a huge net of metro lines has been built over the last 80 years.

C Odd One Out. Circle the word in each group that does not belong.

1 top – above – central – upper
2 place – location – front – spot
3 internal – edge – outside – external

D Now over to You … Answer the questions using the words from page 108.

1 Describe the house you live in. In which area is it? Is it near the city centre?
What is in front of the house and around it?
2 What are your favourite spots in your home town? What makes them so special to you?
3 Do you prefer to do things inside or outside? Which locations do you prefer?

Colours

When the traffic light turns *green*, you can go. When the traffic light turns *red*, the cars have to stop. A *white* car stops because the traffic light shows a *red* light.

Peter's Life

Peter's hobby is his car. He has been working on it for hours. Now his hands are *black* with oil. A normal room has four *corners*. One room in Peter's house is rather unusual. It has five *corners*. Peter met his wife Sarah in college. *Both* of them got their MA in the same year. Susan and Peter went on holiday *together*. That was when they decided to marry. They got a cake in the *shape* of a heart for the wedding. Peter is a minister. He has even met the Dalai Lama, who is a leading *figure* of Buddhism. Due to his position, Peter has a lot of duties which *include* his presence at official dinners. Peter has two brothers. One is a doctor and the *other* one has not finished high school yet.

Different Continents

Annie is going to spend her holiday in Africa, where the sky is *blue* with *white* clouds. After three days under the hot African sun, Annie's skin is burnt. She now looks *red* like a tomato. Annie saw a zebra for the first time in her life. Wondering about its strange *pattern*, she was *not* sure if it is a *black* animal with *white* stripes or a *white* animal with *black* stripes. Annie has already visited a lot of beautiful places, but her guide tells her that there are still *other* and more beautiful sites to see. In the village next to the hotel, all *kinds* of fruits and drinks are sold. All houses in the village are built without *corners*. They are completely *round*. Annie is *not* familiar with the African culture. This is why she often wonders about the strange behaviour of the people. The swimming pool at her hotel looks strange, it has the *form* of a banana. Back in Europe, returning to her daily routine is *not as* easy *as* Annie imagined.

Common Terms

- Jack is very good at learning languages. He can speak more than five *different* languages.
- A *square* is a figure with four *corners* and four sides. All sides have the same length.
- You can draw a *square* with only four *lines*.
- In traditional Irish dancing the dancers often form a *circle* or a *line*.
- I do not have a lot of time. Would you please come to the *point* of your statement?
- '*Too*' is another term for 'also' or 'as well'. She married last year and her brother will marry this year, *too*.

A A New Car. Rewrite the underlined phrases using one of the following words. Sometimes you need to change the sentence structure or the word order.

kind ▪ too ▪ included ▪ both ▪ shape ▪ as

1 The car my father bought last year looks really strange: it has the form of an egg.
2 He was promised that the car would be lightning fast.
3 In the price for the car was all extra equipment my father wanted.
4 When I saw the car, I really liked it. My mother also really liked it.
5 The two of us did not want the car, but my father would not listen to us.
6 After all, my father has always been that sort of man who enjoys extravagant things.

B Associations. Which colours do you associate with these nouns?

1	blue	a	leafs on a tree
2	red	b	winter
3	green	c	blood
4	black	d	the night
5	white	e	the sky

C At the Gallery. Complete the sentences using the following words.

colours ▪ patterns ▪ not ▪ other ▪ figure ▪ different ▪ together ▪ points ▪ round

1 Last month there was an exhibition at an art gallery. Linda and Jenny decided to go there ______________.
2 The famous paintings came from ______________ countries all around the world.
3 Jenny saw a painting by Vincent van Gogh, a very famous ______________ in the history of art.
4 The painting showed flowers in the artist's room in bright ______________.
5 There was another painting of Joan Miró with a strange design of different ______________.
6 Two artists were invited to the exhibition. One of them presented his work. The ______________ one did not appear.
7 Jenny nearly fell into a ______________ hole in the ground which in fact was an abstract work of art.
8 The exhibition was so big that the visitors could ______________ see everything in one day.
9 There is also a presentation by a professor tomorrow. He will talk about important ______________ in the history of art.

D Now over to You … Answer the questions using the words from page 110.

1 Which shapes do you know from geometry?
2 In which everyday objects can you find these shape?
3 Name your favourite colours.
4 What do you possess in these colours?

A Cheap Copy

Tim and Paul live next to each other. They have *similar* houses. The only *difference* is that Tim's house has more windows than Paul's house.

You do not have to be an expert to recognise that this picture of the "Mona Lisa" is merely a cheap *copy* of the original painting.

At the Shop

The new shop which opened two weeks ago is really huge. It offers a great *variety* of all kinds of things you can possibly think of. In *contrast* to all other shops, it does not close until 10 o'clock in the evening.
The new shop *belongs* to a big company which has its main shop in France. The company's aims are offering a *combination* of good quality and a huge selection of items. The shop itself is *divided* into different sections. Each section contains a different selection of items. The supermarket is *separate* from other buildings, so you can already see it from far away. Another *advantage* of the new supermarket is its position. From any spot of the city it will only take you ten minutes to reach it. They sell all *sorts* of food. It was *sort of* difficult for me to decide what to buy. *Like* my mother used to say: sometimes less is more.

A New Version

- I am one of those people who like to go out and eat in a good restaurant. This *sort* of person is rare in my city. Some might say that this is wasting money.
- Mary tries to find a job *elsewhere*, because she does not like the job she has right now.
- She hopes to find a job, where she can *combine* business with pleasure.
- The enterprises should not make a *distinction* between women and men. They should treat them equally.
- Jenny's house and mine are very *similar*. They just *vary* in the colour: hers is green and mine is white.
- My mother always *compares* the prices of the products and tries to buy the cheapest one.

Two Writers

Being a writer, John has been living in *relatively* poor conditions for several years. His wife Linda is a writer *as well*. But she prefers to call herself an artist. John did not go to university. *Neither* did Linda. Nevertheless, they have spent a lot of time studying and reading books on their own. John's decision to become a writer was rather clear. He could not think of anything else. His parents tried to persuade him to have a *common* job like manager or officer but he refused to. Although John and Linda *both* love to read, they prefer *different types* of books. Last week both of them began writing short texts for a writing competition. This has led to some arguments and has caused a *division* between them. After two weeks of work, John and Linda present the final *version* of their texts at the competition. It soon becomes clear that *either* John or Linda is going to win the competition. Despite *variations* concerning the style and theme of John's and Linda's text, both are good enough to win the first prize.

A Preparing Lunch. Replace the underlined words with the following words.

relative ▪ variety ▪ varies ▪ combined ▪ type ▪ else ▪ either

1 Every time my brother prepares something for lunch, the quality of it changes a lot.
2 Last week he put together old fruits with other strange things because he wanted to try something new.
3 He often asks me what other things he could use to make his meals more interesting.
4 I tell him as one possibility to create something special and to eat it alone or to stick to traditional meals which all of us could enjoy.
5 My father also likes to prepare lunch for the family. The only problem is that he only knows how to prepare one kind of meal.
6 Compared to what my father does, my brother's skills can be called special.
7 I finally decided to take my lunch in the restaurant next to our house. They offer a great range of nice meals.

B Odd One Out. Circle the word in each group that does not belong.

1 separate – contrast – combination – divide
2 to compare – neither – as well – sort of
3 elsewhere – version – variation – sort

C Crossword. Complete the crossword puzzle using the clues provided.

Across:
1 When something is separated
5 The recognizing or noting of differences
9 A number of different types of things

Down:
2 Different form of something
3 Another word for benefit, gain or profit
4 An instance or point of unlikeness or dissimilarity
6 Having a likeness or resemblance
7 Occurring frequently
8 An imitation, reproduction, or transcript of an original

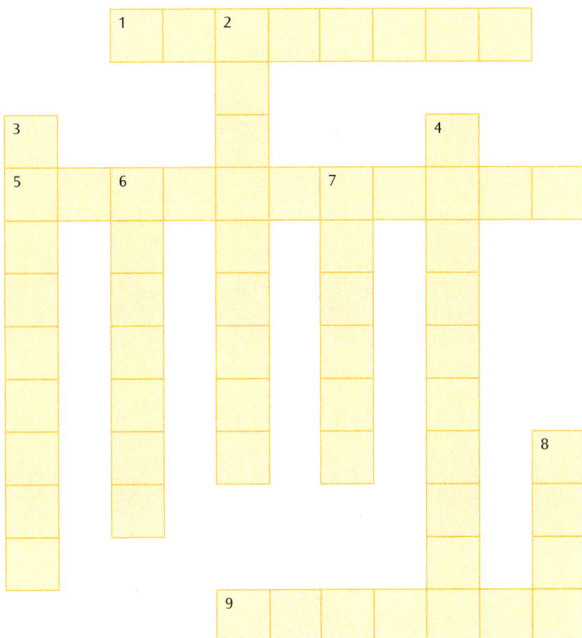

D Either … Or. Put the following words in order from similar to different.

distinction ▪ common ▪ like ▪ variation ▪ difference

____

E Now over to You … Answer the questions using the words from page 112.

1 Do you know any countries or cities which are or have been divided in the recent past? Have you ever visited one of them? What do you know about them or what have you seen there?
2 Do you have brothers or sisters? Are their characters rather similar or different from yours? Give some examples.
3 You are studying a foreign language. Describe what sort of advantage you expect this to bring you in the future. In what kind of situations do you think your knowledge will prove to be useful?

Exciting Events

When the film reached the *end*, my grandfather remained in his seat. He had fallen asleep.

Aunt Mary

My Aunt Mary does the weather programme for a popular TV station. The weather forecast is shown *twice* a day: in the morning and in the evening. Whenever I meet her, Aunt Mary talks a lot about the weather. Thus I always know what the weather will be like the *next* days. I *often* ask my aunt to talk about something else than the weather. She will then start to talk about the global atmosphere and its influence ... on the weather, of course. When Aunt Mary graduated from university, she began working for the TV station on a *regular* basis. *Last* week she said it would rain for five days, which it actually did. The last *sequence* of the weather programme is always the same. My aunt stands in front of a map and smiles into the camera. It never *occurred* to my aunt to do anything else but the weather programme. Even as a little girl she used to stand outside and look into the sky. Recently, Aunt Mary has been voted to be the *fourth* most popular personality on TV. The first three are well-known actors. I suppose my aunt will *continue* doing the weather programme until she is a hundred years old.

Preparing for a Test

My exam this week will be on the environmental problems in Indonesia and their *implications* for the region. I have already read the first 15 chapters in a book on this subject. However, the chapters were so difficult that I had to read them *again*. I needed a good knowledge about them to understand the *following* part of the book: chapters 16–30. One implication of environmental problems is the increasing amount of disease in children. There is *also* an increasing amount of people formerly living in villages who want to live in the cities now. The *latter* point concerns regions all over the world. There is a *link* between the environment and the economy: the bad economic situation *caused* by environmental problems forces people to leave their villages.

Fair Play

Ron is playing rugby for a local club. He will play in today's *opening* match of the season. As Ron is tall and rather heavy, his coach decided that he should play in the defence, which is his *usual* position in the matches. In the *previous* season Ron and his club did not win the regional championship. This was due to a *series* of injuries among the most important players of the club. The club is being supported by a number of local companies such as: the filling station, the Chinese restaurant, *etc*. For Ron, playing rugby is closely *linked* with his childhood. He has played rugby since he was eight. In the *second* half of today's match, Ron scored two goals. In the end, Ron's team was *ahead* by five points and won the match.

A Who Is First? Organise the following words into categories according to their meaning and add other words and expressions you know.

last ▪ first ▪ series ▪ latter ▪ third ▪ regular ▪ second ▪ fourth ▪ previous ▪ to continue

B Go for the Gold. Replace the underlined words with the following opposite words.

end ▪ often ▪ next ▪ usual ▪ opening

1 The president ended the closing ceremony with the words: “Let the games begin.”
2 China will take part in this international competition. This nation is rarely seen in this kind of event.
3 It is unusual for the British team to win a lot of competitions.
4 The previous race in this competition is well-known by all nations.
5 In the beginning, all nations were quite content with the result of the competition.

C Opening Sequence. Match the words with their definitions or descriptions.

1	sequence	a	further advanced in time or number
2	to occur	b	a connection of two or more things
3	again	c	to come to one’s mind
4	link	d	particular order of numbers or events
5	ahead	e	short form for ‘and others’
6	etc	f	one more time

D Linking Letters. Find six words from this chapter in the word search.

V	S	E	F	G	E	N	D	O	R	W
I	M	L	O	D	S	E	E	R	C	J
S	H	S	L	J	I	N	O	L	P	A
I	M	P	L	I	C	A	T	I	O	N
A	O	D	O	T	S	L	I	N	B	R
D	G	N	W	A	A	S	G	K	O	A
N	E	L	I	R	B	O	T	R	E	M
R	F	I	N	I	R	E	N	E	T	I
A	Q	H	G	K	C	A	U	S	E	D

E Now over to You … Answer the questions using the words from page 114.

1 Did you or a friend or family member ever take first, second, or third place in a competition? What kind of competition was it? How old were you (they) then?
2 At the end of one year, many people think about what they hope to achieve within the next year. What goals have you set for yourself? Did you succeed in your purpose?

Quite All Right

The party I went to yesterday was rather *formal*. Not being dressed *appropriately* gave me an uncomfortable feeling.

At the Game Show

Jenny was chosen to take part in a TV game show. In the game show, the candidates can choose between different *categories* of questions. Jenny is pretty *sure* that she is going to win today's show. For the *last* few months she has constantly been studying her books. She has *especially* concentrated on words that start with an 'X'. Jenny has already answered five questions in a *row* but the next question is about sports and sport events. Jenny does not know much about sports *at all* and gives the wrong answer. Nevertheless, before the lights are turned *off* in the studio, Jenny has won a nice sum of money. Jenny already knows *how* to spend the money. She is going to buy some new books.

Different People

- Mary works till 8 pm. She cannot be at the party at 7 o'clock, it is *impossible* for her.
- He is very nice to me but I don't like the way he behaves, I don't like his *manners*.
- You do not see identical twins very *often*; it is a fairly *rare* thing to happen.
- Tim tries to visit his sister once a week. He makes *frequent* visits because he misses her.
- Mary lost her *first* baby, but her *subsequent* pregnancies went well.
- I did not want to bring all the books to my house, so I made a *selection* of the most important ones and left the others at the library.

We Do Need Some Education

Little Timmy *really* hates getting up early in the morning. What he hates even more is getting up early because he has to be in school on time. What he hates *in particular* is getting up early to be in school on time to attend classes. What he hates most is getting up early to be in school on time to attend classes in which he has to do exercises in front of the class ... *and so on*.

Timmy's parents, who are both teachers, constantly explain to him that going to school is a necessary *means* of education. In order to avoid all of this, he shows signs of a severe disease on *occasional* mornings. Timmy is *quite* convincing when he pretends to be ill. That is why he was taken to the doctor's several times and missed his classes. Nevertheless, Timmy's parents know that he *tends* to change his mind quite often. In a few years Timmy might even like going to school.

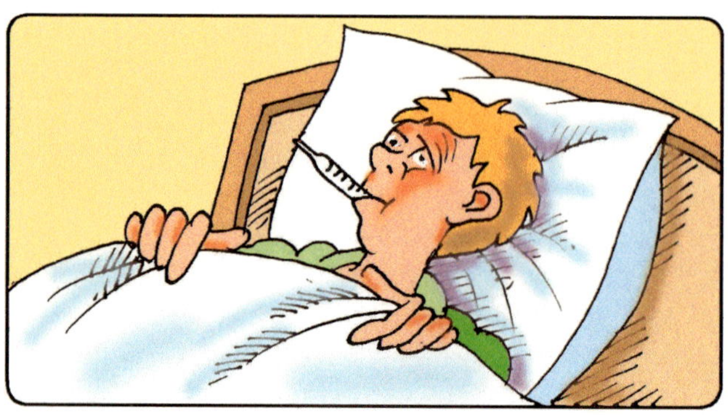

A Bad Manners. Match the words with their definitions or descriptions.

1	category	a	a system or action which serve a purpose
2	manner	b	a series of things or people with a connection
3	how	c	to a certain degree
4	to tend	d	at the end of a list for things which have not been mentioned
5	chain	e	another word for especially
6	means	f	a group of people or things with common features
7	in particular	g	asking for the way or manner
8	quite	h	the way something is done or happening
9	and so on	i	to be used to act in a particular way

B My Best Friend. Replace the underlined words with the following words.

rare ▪ at all ▪ sure ▪ off ▪ on ▪ frequent ▪ impossible ▪ appropriate

1 John used to be a good friend. Whenever I had lost all hope he told me that nothing was possible.
2 John became a rare visitor over the last few years. We saw each other several times a week.
3 When we met we usually listened to music. My parents came to my room occasionally to tell me that I should turn the music on.
4 I invited John to my mother's birthday. When he appeared in a suit and a tie I had to admit that he was dressed in a manner that was not suitable for the occasion.
5 I was uncertain that John and I would be best friends for the rest of our lives.
6 But one day he found some letters off my table which the person he loved had written to me.
7 In fact, Mary, John's girlfriend, had written them to me but I had not answered them a lot.
8 From then on John's visits became frequent until he stopped visiting me for good.

C Means and Methods. Match the following words with the pictures.

rare ▪ formal ▪ selection ▪ row

1 ____________________

2 ____________________

3 ____________________

4 ____________________

D Now over to You … Answer the questions using the words from page 116.

1 Describe what you do frequently, rarely, never, on weekends and during the week.
2 Imagine a rather formal occasion. Which dress, manner or behaviour is considered appropriate where you come from?
3 Do you consider the Internet an appropriate and sufficient means to inform yourself? Name at least three alternative sources of information and discuss the advantages of each medium.

Ultimate Experience

When my brother and I were children our father used to sit in the *middle* of us and read books to us.

Peter is *wasting* his money for things he will never use. It is as though he is throwing it away.

Paris

Annie's parents returned from their trip to Paris. They tell their daughter about the *great* attractions of the city. They went to the Louvre and found all the paintings quite *interesting*. From the top of the Eiffel Tower they had a *perfect* view of the city. They visited Montmartre and enjoyed the *lovely* atmosphere. Each day they had a *wonderful* lunch in their hotel which consisted of fresh bread with cheese and *excellent* salad. Some people do not like the strong and rather *bad* smell of French Camembert. Annie's parents loved it from the start. Before leaving for their trip, Annie's parents bought a city map which turned out to be quite *useful*. They were advised not to stay in certain parts of the city which were considered not to be *safe*. After listening to her parents' stories for days, Annie got a *slight* pain in her head whenever the word 'Paris' was mentioned. In addition, her parents have started arguing about the *correct* way to prepare a 'Ratatouille'.

Of Good Quality

- The most *effective* way to lose weight is to eat less and exercise more.
- The test was really *difficult* and a lot of pupils failed.
- I do not have enough money. Because I *lack* money I cannot even buy food.
- Mike does not like Mondays because he *hates* to get up so early and go to work.
- Look at this sentence. It is not *correct*: there is a *wrong* word in it.
- If you work in a bank, you have to be very *exact*. There should not be any money missing.
- A *standard* is a commonly-accepted level of *quality* or behaviour.
- The material of these clothes is so *fine* that I only wear them when there are special events.
- When I finished university I had problems with the *practical* work because I only knew the theory.

The New Product

Ladies and Gentlemen, I am *very* glad to welcome you here today to present our new product. It is without a doubt the *ultimate* improvement to all existing products on the market. It has passed various tests under *extreme* conditions. It is *well*-known that our standards are beyond existing limits by far. Developing our new product, we made it a *priority* to create something completely new. The *good* quality of our products is being confirmed daily by millions of happy users. Our new product has various uses. It is *suitable* to cope with almost every existing problem. Our new product is so *easy* to use that even a child could handle it since we added a security system. According to the numbers of last year, 98% of our costumers have had only *positive* experiences with our products. The remaining two percent might not have used the product in the *right* way.

A Excellent Quality. Unscramble the groups of letters to form the words described in the sentences.

1 DLDEMI ____________________: placed with equal distance to both ends

2 TIORPIYR ____________________: things to be done first

3 TECFIFVEE ____________________: producing the desired results

4 YAES ____________________: not difficult

5 RITNEENSGTI ____________________: attracting your attention so that you want to know more about it

6 HIGRT ____________________: not wrong

7 LTUITMAE ____________________: being the best or most extreme

8 CAXTE ____________________: being very precise

9 ROECRCT ____________________: being accurate

B Odd One Out. Circle the word in each group that does not belong.

1 excellent – bad – perfect – wonderful
2 practical – useful – difficult – suitable
3 great – fine – slight – well
4 standard – good – quality – wrong

C Bad Influence. Determine whether each sentence is a true statement or a false one. For false sentences, provide a correct alternative.

		T	F
1	To waste means to keep things with value.	☐	☐
2	The middle is the place on the left end of an object.	☐	☐
3	Positive is something which is considered to be good.	☐	☐
4	Practical things can be used well.	☐	☐
5	If you lack something you have too much of it.	☐	☐
6	Extreme means that something is normal.	☐	☐
7	The word ‘very’ is used to put emphasis on a word.	☐	☐
8	When something is a priority it is very important.	☐	☐

E Now over to You … Answer the questions using the words from page 118.

1 Is quality an important factor for you when you buy things? Are you willing to spend more money for things of high quality or do you think that is wasting money? Explain why.
2 Describe something beautiful you have seen. What impressed you about it?
3 If you want to sell something, how can you persuade somebody that the product has great characteristics?

A Hot Day

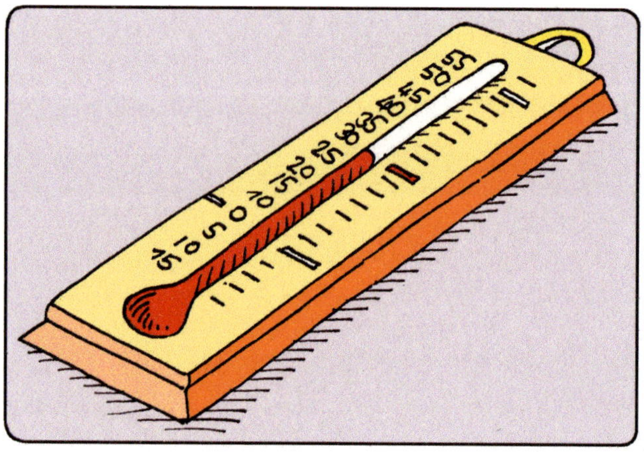

Today is a very hot day. The temperature is expected to reach 30 *degrees*.

A Visit to New York

After Paul's arrival in the city of New York, his *prime* concern was to find a place to stay. Since Paul came to the city in August, it was *apparent* to him that this could be a problem. Paul's *main criterion* for choosing a hotel in New York City was the price. Hotels can be *quite* expensive. It was not easy to find one that was *alright* but did not cost too much. The *key* reason for tourists to visit New York is the variety the city has to offer. Paul visited the Empire State Building first. From the *top* of that famous building he had a great view of the city. Every year thousands of people visit the museums in New York. The Guggenheim, for example, has a *constant* number of visitors and can be quite crowded.

Saving the Earth

Pollution has *severe* effects on our environment: trees are dying and rivers run dry. A number of *critical* reports claim that our species is constantly contributing to destroying itself. Most of those reports conclude that a change of our behaviour is an *inevitable* step to save our planet.
To implement important changes is the *overall* responsibility of everybody. One *significant* change is to walk or use public transportation instead of cars. Another important step would be to replace nuclear energy with *alternative* energies like wind or water. The increasing demand for energy is a *major* factor for the critical situation. Many politicians are *pretty* sure that action to save the earth has to be taken immediately; otherwise it will be too late. They developed a plan to improve the situation. The most important *stage* is to make people more environmentally aware. The *importance* of political action in this area cannot be questioned.

Justice for All

Chris works as a lawyer. His *main* occupation consists of talking with clients or defending them in court. On a *typical* working day he leaves the house at eight o'clock in the morning and returns at six o'clock in the evening. As justice is the most *essential* value of society for him, he decided to study law. During his first two years at university he picked up *basic* knowledge which turned out to be very important for his job. Getting his degree and starting to work was an *absolute* turning point in Chris's life: it seems like everything changed. Back then, his *primary* goal was getting rich as fast as possible. When he realised that he could actually help people, earning money did not seem to be that *relevant* any more. Chris can no longer think of an *alternative* to his current occupation. It is just too satisfying to help people.

A A Severe Illness. Replace the underlined words with the following words.

stages ▪ key ▪ major ▪ degree ▪ critical ▪ constant ▪ typical ▪ alright ▪ severe

1 Paul does not feel well and has been in bed for the last few days. When I asked him about his condition, he said he felt quite <u>okay</u>.
2 As a child, Paul suffered from a <u>serious</u> disease which keeps coming back occasionally.
3 Paul told me that the disease proceeds in three <u>phases</u>.
4 At first he always feels a <u>continuous</u> pain in his neck which will last for some days.
5 Another <u>normal</u> symptom is an increase of temperature, mainly during the night.
6 The disease can also affect other parts of the body, which is considered a <u>big</u> risk.
7 As a child, Paul had already had a <u>dangerous</u> condition when his parents brought him to hospital.
8 The doctor advised Paul to limit his activities to a certain <u>level</u>.
9 He also told Paul that getting some rest would be the <u>solution</u> to recovering his health.

B A Plan for the Future. Complete the sentences using the following words.

importance ▪ main ▪ overall ▪ pretty ▪ basic ▪ primary ▪ essential ▪ relevant ▪ criterion

Linda has just finished school. Now she is checking out all the possibilities ______________ [1] to her interests and her future career. Linda is ______________ [2] sure that she would like to go to university. For her the total or ______________ [3] advantage of studying is the free choice of subjects you can learn. Earning a lot of money and getting rich is of no ______________ [4] to Linda. All she wants is enough money to satisfy her ______________ [5] needs like paying for her room and buying food. There is one ______________ [6] concerning the choice of her future job which Linda considers the most important. Her future job should make her content and happy. This is the most ______________ [7] point in Linda's consideration. Linda visits a university to get more information. After she has met with some students she realises that their ______________ [8] goal is to get a good education. Linda has finally decided what she wants to do. Her ______________ [9] concern now is to start as soon as possible.

C A Critical State. Match the words with their descriptions or definitions.

1	easy to understand → b	a	alternative
2	important enough to be noticed	b	apparent
3	a possibility you can choose instead of something else	c	absolute
4	most important	d	significant
5	another word for 'total'	e	inevitable
6	something that can not be avoided	f	prime

D Now over to You … Answer the questions using the words from page 120.

1 Do you have plans for your future? What are they?
2 How important is money to you?
3 What you are your primary goals in life? What criteria are most important for your future career?

Modern Times

The design of Peter's new car is *modern*.

Tom likes to drive with his window *open*.

The garage door is too *narrow* for Jake's new car.

The Golden Figure

Peter is a private eye. On an *ordinary* day he will sit in his office all day waiting for clients.
But today he is visited by a *strange*-looking man. He gives Peter the task to find a work of art which has disappeared. Peter is not *familiar* with art so he asks the *strange*-looking man to give him more details. He gives Peter a *precise* description of the object he should look for.
Thus Peter learns that he shall look for a figure which is made of *pure* gold. The figure was removed from its *original* location in a museum in London to be part of an exhibition in Germany. On the way to Germany, the figure got lost and was never seen again. It is quite *obvious* that someone took it. The golden figure was secured with a *complex* security system.
Additionally, it was protected by a *thick* sheet of special glass. Peter realises that the solution for this case is rather *simple*. It is quite *clear* that the person which took the figure must have had access to the security system. Therefore, Peter concludes that the he or she has something to do with the museum. It was *okay* that the strange man could not give him any money in advance. He was willing to accept the case anyway. Peter makes an *active* effort. After some days of investigation, it becomes *clear* that the wife of the museum's director took the figure. Strangely enough, Peter found it in her handbag.

Characteristic Features

- The way up the mountain is quite *rough*. It is impossible to go by car or bike. We must walk.
- Thanks, but I can carry my bag by myself. I didn't bring many things, so it is quite *light*.
- A characteristic *feature* of this school is the high discipline of the pupils.
- I don't know the right expression for "I like it more" in German. – Ask your teacher to tell you the *proper* way to say it.

Strange Behaviour

Sarah is a doctor for mental diseases. She has completed *special* training to better deal with patients who suffer from all kinds of mental diseases. Last week Sarah began working in a hospital which offers a *wide* range of possible therapies for people who suffer from mental diseases. Those people are considered "not *normal*" by society. Nevertheless, this type of disease is one of the most frequent in *modern* society. The *characteristics* of mental diseases are quite hard to observe: Sarah's patients often describe it as a general loss of reality. People who are affected by this disease lose contact to *real* events and people around them. Most of those people cannot escape this bad *condition* without help. After years of work Sarah has developed a *particular* type of programme she uses with her patients. For no *specific* reason this kind of programme seems to work better than those of her colleagues. This is the reason why *new* patients who seek advice keep coming to her.

A Clear Conditions. Match the words with their definitions or descriptions.

1 strange
2 new
3 obvious
4 active
5 open
6 simple
7 characteristics
8 proper
9 feature

a things that set somebody or something apart
b the opposite of difficult
c not closed
d a normal characteristic of something
e the opposite of old
f easy to understand or to see
g being busy with something
h appropriate or correct
i being not usual or normal

B Word Search. Find eight words from this chapter in the word search.

S	A	S	D	F	M	G	H	J	K	L	C
P	N	A	R	R	O	W	Y	X	C	V	O
E	R	F	V	B	D	N	B	V	C	M	M
C	T	G	B	N	E	Z	N	H	Z	G	P
I	D	S	E	D	R	G	F	H	R	O	L
F	E	D	R	F	N	O	R	M	A	L	E
I	T	G	Z	H	U	J	I	K	O	I	X
C	F	A	M	I	L	I	A	R	L	G	M
J	U	H	Z	G	T	F	D	R	E	H	N
D	F	R	B	H	U	J	G	F	E	T	G
P	A	R	T	I	C	U	L	A	R	D	R

C My Father. Replace the underlined words with the following opposite words.

ordinary ▪ special ▪ rough ▪ precise ▪ clear ▪ original ▪ real ▪ wide ▪ thick

1 My father has been working on a ship for a long time. The sun and wind made his skin become dark and soft.
2 Working on a ship is hard work. This is why my father's arms were so thin.
3 My father often tells me great stories about what he has seen and the places he has been to. I always thought all he said was made up.
4 He told me that he had once acquired the copy of a famous painting for only one dollar.
5 He also gave me a rough description of an animal with two heads which he had seen once.
6 His body has amazing capacities. On a(n) strange day he will have up to ten meals.
7 The door to his apartment is very narrow. His massive body would get stuck otherwise.
8 The things he told me always seemed to be very difficult to me. I think I have learned a lot about life just by listening to my father.
9 My father will always remain one of the most normal people to me. Nevertheless, I know that he sometimes adds details to the truth.

D Now over to You … Answer the questions using the words from page 122.

1 Describe your room with respect to its structure and size.
2 List some characteristics of the following things: water, wood, metal.

At the Bus Stop

Many people have to *wait* because the bus is *late*.

Mr. Smith can *no longer wait* for the bus and calls a taxi instead.

Time Is Money

Time is very important to John. His day is very organised. John is *always* on *time*. Every morning he arrives at his work place 30 minutes before he has to start work. He prefers to be *early* rather than *late*. When he is *early*, he has some time to prepare himself for the day. His colleagues have *never* seen him be *late*. He has not been *late* once. He is *still* the only person in the company who has not been *late* or sick for five years. However, *today* everything is different. John has not arrived at the office. This is the first time that John is *late* for work. His colleagues worry about him. For a *moment* they think that something might have happened to him. *When* he finally calls the office to say that his car was stolen and he will take a bus to work, everybody is relieved. *Now* they can all go back to work.

Going to the Doctor

Ben: Have you *ever* had to *wait* less than an hour at the doctor's office?
Sara: Not *yet*. But I hope that I won't have to *wait* so long at this new doctor's across the street.
Ben: *Then* you know what I mean.
Sara: Oh, yes indeed. *Sometimes*, when I am tired of *waiting*, I leave for half an hour to go for a walk and *then* return. But I don't do that very often.
Ben: That is a great idea. I may also *eventually* switch doctors. Then I could go somewhere closer.
Sara: Oh, we'll have to talk again *later*. I have an appointment at the doctor's. I will call you *when* I get home.
Ben: I hope you will only have to *wait* for a little *while*.

The New Library

A lot of people were *present* to celebrate the opening of the new library. About 500 people came during the day. The *actual* number of people was 498. At the beginning, the president of the library held an *initial* speech. He *started* with talking about the importance of libraries as a place of education. He also explained the *circumstances* that had caused the building of a new library. There had been a fire which had destroyed the old library. His *final* comment was about raising money to build a nice coffee shop next to the library. When he *finished* his speech, most people were smiling and very happy.

A Sarah's Birthday Party. Correct the following sentences.

always ▪ early ▪ eventually ▪ late ▪ never ▪ no longer ▪ still ▪ today

1. Yesterday is Sarah's birthday.
2. Sarah is hardly happy on this special day.
3. She loves to get up late in the morning. At 6 o'clock her parents are still in bed and she can open her presents all by herself.
4. She really wants to have a party in the evening like all the years before.
5. She likes to start not too early in the evening, so that she can have a really long party.
6. Sarah tried to convince her parents to pay for a well-known DJ to play music at her party. They immediately agreed.
7. Sarah always has problems persuading her parents.
8. The party is something that Sarah will no longer remember, even as she gets older.

B Talking to a Friend. Replace the underlined words with the following words.

circumstance ▪ later ▪ now ▪ present ▪ then ▪ when ▪ yet

Mark: Hey, Peter. Is it true that you like the fact[1] that your teacher is your father's best friend?
Peter: Of course I do. I would not be passing math class at the moment[2] if Mr Jones had not helped me a bit.

Mary: Hi Susan, would you like to go swimming?
Susan: Not right now. How about if we go in two hours[3]?
Mary: But at that time[4] the sun will be gone.

Jenny: At what time[5] are we going out?
Michael: Not too early. If we go to the night club before eleven o'clock, there won't be anybody there[6].

Linda: Have you called your mother by now[7]?
George: No, but don't worry. I will do it later.

C Time. Organise the words into pairs.

moment ▪ to finish ▪ initial ▪ final ▪ to start ▪ while

D Now over to You … Answer the questions using the words from page 124.

1. How important is time to you? Are you a person who is very organised and always on time?
2. Tell us about your family and friends. Do you know somebody who is always late? What does this person say about being late?
3. Would you like to live in a place where time is not important at all? What would be different?

General Time

morning

night

The family watches TV in the *evening*.

During the *day*, the children play in the park.

The Car Accident

George drove home from work. He was so tired that he closed his eyes for a *brief* moment. He thought that he had closed his eyes only for a second. But then there was a *sudden* noise and George realised that he had hit the car in front of him. Everything happened very quickly. When George stopped the car, he was *still* very confused. Neither the person in the other car nor he moved. After a short *period* of time, George understood what had happened and got out of his car. He had only stayed for a few seconds in his car. When he saw that the other person was hurt he called the police. His *immediate* reaction saved the other person's life. At *present*, George prefers to take the bike. After the accident he stopped driving.

Divisions of Time

- The concert *lasted* only 30 minutes because the singer felt sick and had to go back to his hotel. Even though it did not *last* very long, people had a good *time*.
- One *hour* before Mary was to get married nobody could find her future husband. This was the longest *hour* she experienced in her life.
- This *week* Chris can stay at home. It is the *week* of the Christmas holidays.
- The *year* 1989 was special in Germany. It was the *year* when the Berlin Wall came down.
- In *January*, John makes plans for the new *year*.
- *Spring time* officially begins in the *month* of *March*.
- The weather in *April* changes a lot. Annie doesn't like to have her birthday in *April*. She never knows if the weather will be nice and if she can have a garden party.
- Her friend Susan was born one *month* later, in *May*, when the weather is usually a lot nicer.
- Mark was born in *June*, when it is usually warm enough to have a pool party on his birthday.

Time Frame

- After finishing school, most students experience a *phase* of freedom. It is a *time* where many students like to travel.
- Sarah's *prospects* of recovery after the treatment are very good. The doctor told her that she would not have any further problems.
- The interview lasted 155 *minutes*. The film star would not stop talking.
- The 18th *century* was the *century* of the French Revolution.
- The 25th of *December* is a very important *date* to many people.
- The spring *term* at German universities starts in *April* and ends in *July*.

A Day or Night. Replace the underlined words with the following opposite words.

brief ▪ day ▪ evening ▪ morning ▪ night ▪ present

1 Mark prefers to work in the <u>morning</u>. He likes to sleep in and start working later.
2 During the <u>day</u>, everything was quiet. There were no people in the dark streets.
3 Annie loves to stay home in the <u>evening</u> when everyone else has gone to work. That is the only time when she has the house all to herself.
4 Peter was glad that most of his friends were <u>gone</u> in class.
5 For a <u>long</u> moment Michael did not know what to do.
6 During the <u>night</u>, Ron did all his homework for the next week.

B Life after School. Complete the sentences using the following words.

immediate ▪ last ▪ period ▪ time ▪ months ▪ phase ▪ prospects ▪ term

1 The last ______________ of school is always very hard.
2 It is a ______________ of time when most students are looking forward to finishing school.
3 Even though not all of them have the same ______________ of finding a good job, most of them are optimistic.
4 The school year will be over in a week. It will not ______________ much longer.
5 Those who go to college or university enter a different ______________ of life.
6 There is no need for an ______________ decision.
7 The students have some ______________ to make their decision.
8 University does not start until a few ______________ later.

C Time Divisions. Match the words with their definitions or descriptions.

1	century → c	a	something that happens quickly and without warning
2	minute	b	specific day of a month
3	hour	c	lasts 100 years
4	sudden	d	lasts 60 minutes
5	date	e	lasts 60 seconds
6	year	f	has 12 months

D Now over to You … Answer the questions using the words from page 126.

1 What is your favourite time of day? Are you a morning or an evening person? Why?
2 Describe your favourite month. Do you prefer summer or winter months?
3 How would you describe the phase of life you are in right now? What are your prospects? Do you have plans for your future?

The Four Seasons

spring

summer

fall

winter

One Week in Paul's Life

Paul loves *Fridays*. It is his favourite day of the *week*. On *Friday*, he finishes work earlier. Instead of coming home in the *evening*, he gets home in the *afternoon*. Then he still has a lot of time to read the newspaper and play with his children before dinner. He can't wait for the *weekend*. During the *weekend*, Paul enjoys his days off. On *Saturday*, he loves to go shopping. It is the only *day* of the *week* when he doesn't have to work and all shops are open. On *Sunday* he goes to church because his wife likes to go there. *Sunday* is also the *day* when he goes for a walk with the dog. Like many other people, Paul does not like *Mondays*. *Monday* is the *day* of the *week* when work begins.

Talking about the Weather

Paul: Jenny, what is your favourite *month* of the *year*?
Jenny: Oh, I love *September*, when it is still warm outside but *fall* is near.
Paul: Mmh, I guess I prefer *December*. In *December* it's Christmas. What could be better?
Jenny: Yes, but I am talking about the *season* and not about holidays. I thought you meant the weather.
Paul: Oh, I see. Well, then I prefer *July*. It's in the middle of the *year* and it's *summer*!
Jenny: I totally agree. I also love *summer*. I think *August* is also wonderful.
Paul: What about *winter*? *January* is just great. It's the first *month* of the *year*.
Jenny: Yes, *January* is all right. I also like *February*. There's so much snow and you can go skiing.
Paul: And *October*? It's Halloween in *October*!
Jenny: I don't know. It's ok. For me it's not very different from *November*. It's cold outside but usually there isn't a lot of snow. There's Thanksgiving, though. I guess I prefer the *months* of the *year* when it's either really warm or really cold.

Making an Appointment

Annie: It's been a *decade* since we finished school. Ten *years* is a long time. We should organise a get-together with our former fellow students.
Sarah: Oh, I know. But we already have an *annual* class meeting. Don't you think one party a *year* is enough?
Annie: No, I don't. There's always a reason to party. I could meet with old friends *daily* and talk about the good old times.
Sarah: Well, what about *tonight* then? We could have a small party on our own.
Annie: You are funny. In the *beginning* you tell me you think that there are too many parties and in the end you want one *tonight*?
Sarah: If *tonight* is too soon for you we can have one *tomorrow* night!
Annie: You are crazy!

A Networks. What do you associate with the four seasons? Use words from page 128 and add more words you know.

spring **summer** **fall** **winter**

B Divisions of Time. Match the words with their definitions or descriptions.

1	annual → e	a	something that happens every day
2	beginning	b	the first day of the week
3	decade	c	the two days of the week when most people do not have to work
4	daily	d	a period of the year with special events
5	weekend	e	something that happens once a year
6	Monday	f	the start of something
7	season	g	a period of ten years

C Going on a Date. Complete the sentences using the following words.

afternoon ▪ Friday ▪ Saturday ▪ Sunday ▪ tomorrow ▪ tonight

Michael: Susan, would you like to go out with me ____________________[1]?

Susan: Oh, I'm sorry. How about ____________________[2]?

Michael: You always say that. But all right, when should I pick you up?

Susan: In the ____________________[3]. Let's say at 3 o'clock.

Michael: That's not a real date! I want to go out at night!

Susan: Michael, I already have a date on ____________________[4] night. It's the first night of the weekend.

Michael: But I wanted to go to this party with you. There is no party on ____________________[5]. Do you want us to go to church together instead?

Susan: Ok, ok. So, why don't we go out next ____________________[6] night? I am flying to Paris with John for the weekend. So we can meet the night before.

Michael: Hmm. I guess I just have to find a girl who is not as popular as you.

D Now over to You … Answer the questions using the words from page 128.

1. What is your favourite season of the year? Why do you prefer this time to other times of the year? Which month do you like most?
2. What do you do during the week? Do you have hobbies which you do regularly? Describe a typical week.
3. Have you ever planned a big meeting? How did you manage to find a date where most people had time? How long did you spend on planning the meeting?

Today and Tomorrow

This is what cars looked like in *former* times.

This is what a car in *recent* times looks like.

This is what a *future* car might look like.

Future Technologies

Jane is involved in research about *potential* energy sources. She thinks there are a lot of *potential* ways to produce energy besides burning oil. Since oil is becoming less and less available, we *certainly* have to find new ways to obtain energy. She says that it is *unlikely* that cars will need gas in the *future*. One *possibility* of producing energy is using water power. Another *possibility* is using wind power. It is possible that in the *future* we will not depend on oil any more, but rather benefit from the sun's energy. It is already *possible* to use waves to generate electricity. Jane says that one day it will be *possible* to obtain energy from waste.

Historical Interest

Peter is interested in *ancient* cultures, for example *ancient* Rome or *ancient* Greece. Last summer Peter visited Italy because of his interest in *history*. In Italy he went to museums every day. Peter has been interested in *historical* matters for more than five years now. Since he visited Rome, his *historical* interest has increased. He is especially interested in the politics of the *past*. Peter thinks that the *past* can teach us a lot for today. Sometimes people wonder why Peter is interested in something that happened 2000 years *ago*. He says that looking *back* at ancient Rome is a good way of understanding the mechanisms of today's politics. When we look *back* we can learn from *history*. Peter *derives* patterns for the rise and fall of dictators from Rome's *history*. For example: *once* Caesar was dead, Rome broke down. But *once* Octavian became emperor, Rome became powerful again. Why was that?

Only Five More Minutes

John: Linda, it is 11pm *already*, please let us go home. I have *already* called a taxi.

Linda: Okay, John, we will go *soon*. Only five more minutes.

John: You said we would go home *earlier* than usual today. Did you forget that I have to get up *earlier* than you tomorrow morning?

Linda: Yes, yes, we will go *soon*. Only five more minutes.

John: Linda, *before* we went to the party you promised we would not stay long. Do you even remember what you said *before*? It is past midnight now! I want to leave!

Linda: Okay, John. Only five more minutes.

John: Oh Linda! If only *once* we could go home early. *Perhaps* I should not have come with you to a party on Monday night in the first place. *Maybe* I had better go home alone now and you can stay as long as you want. Good night!

A Do Not Look Back. Replace the underlined words with the following opposite words.

back ▪ earlier ▪ former ▪ future ▪ possible ▪ recent ▪ unlikely

1 My future girlfriend was a doctor.
2 I was hurt when she left me. I decided not to look forward any more.
3 I think everything was better later.
4 It is impossible to lose two pounds per week.
5 To eat bananas only is a very old method to lose weight.
6 In the past I will exercise more.
7 It is likely that through eating healthily I will gain weight.

B Odd One Out. Circle the word in each group that does not belong.

1 historical – ancient – the past – future
2 likely – certainly – perhaps – possibility
3 ago – yesterday – soon – once

C What Will Be Next? Replace the underlined words with the following words.

already ▪ derive ▪ history ▪ maybe ▪ once ▪ past ▪ potential

1 Have you turned in your paper yet?
2 One time in my life I want to go to Alaska.
3 Perhaps Linda can help you.
4 It is already twenty minutes after one o'clock!
5 I think she is the possible next president of the USA.
6 Peter wants to obtain knowledge from his research.
7 Mike studies the former times of Europe.

D Word Scramble. Find eight words from this chapter in the word search.

Q	W	S	E	R	R	T	H	Z
A	G	O	D	S	E	A	I	U
B	N	O	M	K	C	Y	S	I
Q	A	N	C	I	E	N	T	O
S	D	F	G	H	N	X	O	P
P	A	S	T	V	T	C	R	L
R	U	T	Z	I	O	V	Y	K
B	B	A	C	K	D	F	G	J
C	S	F	U	T	U	R	E	H

E Now over to You ... Answer the questions using the words from page 130.

1 What do you think the weather will be like this weekend? What are your plans?
2 Is there anything you did in the past that you do not want to do in the future? What is it?
3 Are you interested in history? Do you think it is important to look back to what happened in the past? Why?

Let's Compare

Mike has *only* one banana.

Peter has *many* bananas.

John has *more* bananas than Peter, but *less* bananas than Paul.

Paul has the *most* bananas.

This is a *whole* banana. This is not a *whole* banana.

Facts about Bananas

- Out of *all* the different kinds of fruit, bananas are my favourite, because they come in their own package.
- Bananas are *one* of the *most*-sold fruits in the world.
- *Almost all* bananas come from Ecuador or Colombia.
- *Only* one Euro per pound of bananas is not *much*.
- Bananas contain *a lot* of vitamins. They are *very* good for your health.

A Banana Lover

Ron: I eat about ten bananas every week. Every year I eat about 500 bananas in *total*.
Susan: That is a *lot* of bananas! You must like bananas a *lot*.
Ron: *All* my family likes bananas *a lot*. For breakfast, I *only* eat bananas. I like *everything* about bananas, but their colour is especially nice.
Susan: I think you eat too many bananas. You had better *reduce* the amount of bananas you eat by half or you will become the same colour as bananas.
Ron: OK, I will not eat any *more* bananas today.

No Banana Lover

Susan: How about you, Mike? Do you eat as *many* bananas as Ron?
Mike: I do not like bananas *much*. In my *whole* life I have not eaten *more* than five bananas.
Susan: You really do not like bananas? Not even *a bit*? I think there are only a *few* people that do not like bananas.
Mike: No, not even *a bit*. I have not eaten a *single* banana all year. I would not eat even a tiny *bit* of banana, even if I were very hungry.
Susan: You cannot possibly belong to Ron's family!

A Money. Complete the sentences using the following words.

a bit ▪ more ▪ less ▪ more than ▪ much ▪ almost ▪ lot ▪ reduce

1 Since Tim lost his job, he has to ______________ his housing costs.
2 Linda has a better job than Annie. She also earns ______________ Annie.
3 10 000 Euros, that is a ______________ of money!
4 I hope in my next job I will earn ______________ money.
5 Mom, it does not cost that much! – No, Michael, 30 Euros is quite ______________.
6 For five Euros you cannot buy ______________.
7 I want to work ______________ to have more time for my family.
8 I ______________ missed the train this morning.

B All or Nothing. Put the following words in order from small to large amount.

all ▪ few ▪ many ▪ most ▪ single

____

C Amounts. Organise the following words into three categories based on their common meaning.

bit ▪ everything ▪ little ▪ more ▪ the most ▪ much ▪ only ▪ total ▪ whole

D Shopping for Clothes. Choose one of the underlined words to complete the sentences.

1 I like shopping for clothes least of all / very much / most.
2 I go shopping almost every week / almost very day / a few times a year.
3 Last month I spent all / none of / most of my money on clothes.
4 I wish I could spend less money / more money / all my money on clothes.
5 You could say that shopping is my least favourite / only / second favourite hobby.

E Now over to You … Answer the questions using the words from page 132.

1 What do you spend a lot of money on? What do you spend less money on?
2 Where do you live right now? Do you live in a flat or a house? What do you like most about it?
3 Who earns the most money in your family? What do they do?
4 Talk about your food preferences. What do you eat a lot / not at all?

How Big?

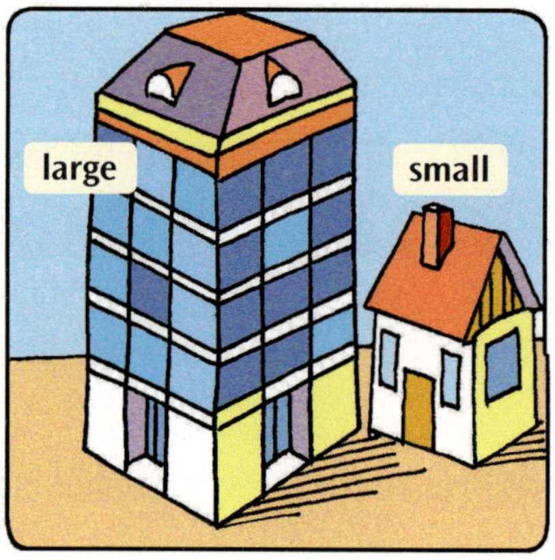

A Change

- There was an *increase* in jobs last year. Because there were *more* jobs, *more* people had work.
- The injury was so bad Susan could *hardly* move her leg. She had to go to the hospital.
- *A lot* of students came to the presentation, so *extra* chairs had to be brought in.
- The temperature was *increasing* every day. It was getting warmer and warmer.
- You can buy a bicycle for *less* money than a car. A car is *more* expensive.
- As Peter's family was eating dinner, the Smith family wanted to join them.
  They had to *add* another table to theirs to make more room.

All

- The *entire* group of boys wanted to see a film. Nobody wanted to do anything else.
- The driver told George that the bus was *full*. There weren't any seats left.
- *Several* people on the plane ordered the fish. Most people ordered the pasta.
- The *total* at the bottom of the bill was a surprise to Annie. It was *a lot* of money.
- Ron's job building the house was *complete*. There was nothing left to do.
- Tom's bank account was *considerable*. He is very rich.
- In mathematics, four quarters make *a whole*.

Some

- Tim ate a *piece* of the pizza for lunch. What he didn't eat he gave to his brother.
- The game system cost $300. Tim only had a *mere* 30 cents.
- John liked to sit in the smoking *section* of the restaurant. John's wife liked the non-smoking part of the restaurant.
- The city zoo *contains many* animals. It also has *many* different kinds of plants.
- Mark got *a little* money from his grandmother for his birthday. He also got some from his parents.
- The dog that Sarah saw in the park today was not the same as the *one* she saw yesterday.
  That *one* was black.
- The *unit* on the third floor is responsible for payments. The group on the fourth floor makes sales.
- At the beach, the *number* of tourists is always high when the weather is good.
- It takes a large *amount* of money to buy an aircraft.

A Some and All. Match the words with their definitions or descriptions.

1 to contain →	a finished, ended
2 unit	b to say more or increase a number
3 complete	c all parts together
4 whole	d with difficulty
5 amount	e to hold inside
6 extra	f groups of things or people
7 to add	g additional, more than normal
8 hardly	h someone, something
9 one	i a quantity, sum

B More and Less. Replace the underlined words with the following opposite words.

large ▪ entire ▪ long ▪ many ▪ a little ▪ full ▪ several ▪ less ▪ increasing

1 Africa is a very <u>small</u> continent.
2 The Nile is a very <u>short</u> river.
3 The <u>incomplete</u> group ate lunch at a restaurant.
4 The glass was <u>empty</u> of water.
5 The temperature was <u>decreasing</u> as the summer started.
6 Poor people have <u>more</u> money than rich people.
7 <u>Many</u> people in the room had blond hair.
8 Ron has <u>much</u> food in the refrigerator.
9 I have <u>few</u> siblings. We are ten children at home.

C And the Rest. Unscramble the groups of letters to fill in the blanks in the sentences.

1 The ________________ CIEEASNR in price made the bread more expensive.

2 Susie's talent is ________________ DRCOIEBNSEAL. She can sing and dance very well.

3 The Pacific Ocean is a very ________________ IGB body of water.

4 The middle ________________ NSETCIO of the train has a restaurant in which you can buy drinks.

5 A very large ________________ RENBUM of people watch television every day.

6 Including the tax, the bill's ________________ LTAOT was well over $100.

7 A teenager is sometimes considered a ________________ EEMR child.

8 The mother gave her son a ________________ IEPCE of chocolate for dessert.

9 My aunt has been ________________ GENISL for all her life.

D Now over to You … Answer the questions using the words from page 134.

1 Describe the city where you live. Have there been any changes in the last ten years?
2 Think back to your childhood. How are you different now than you were then?
3 What are the things you do a lot? What have you never done?

Numbers!

Too Big?

Paul was worried about his *weight*. Most people said he was not too fat or not too thin, but *average*. He was exactly in the middle. He was getting bigger every day, though. His jeans no longer *fit* him. Soon he would have to buy a bigger *size* of jeans. He was gaining almost a *pound* of *weight* a week. He would have to start to eat less.

Size Matters

- A cheeseburger *consists* of meat, cheese and bread.
- The coffee cup was filled to *capacity*. It could not hold anymore.
- John had to *measure* the board so that it was exactly one metre long. Any longer and it would have not been right.
- George wanted to go for a swim, but the swimming pool was *empty*. There was no water in it.
- Jenny's travel bag was much too *heavy*. She couldn't lift it off the ground.
- Chris was unsure of the *content* of the paper bag. He opened it and saw that there were old apples inside.

At School

- *Half* of ten is five.
- One *half* is also 50 *per cent*.
- A dog does not have as much *mass* as a horse. A horse is much bigger.
- The *volume* of a lake is more than the *volume* of a pool. A lake is much bigger than a pool and holds more water.

A Odd One Out. Circle the word in each group that does not belong.

1 ten – two – nine – size
2 weight – heavy – three – pound
3 volume – eight – capacity – measure

B Numbers. Complete the sentences using the following words.

six ▪ percent ▪ half ▪ seven ▪ two ▪ nine ▪ fit ▪ five ▪ four

1 ______________ of eight is four.

2 The human hand has ______________ fingers.

3 There are ______________ days in the week.

4 The year has ______________ seasons.

5 The city had an unemployment rate of eight ______________.

6 On a standard guitar there are ______________ strings.

7 It is very difficult to ______________ more than four people in a small car.

8 Eight divided by ______________ is four.

9 Three multiplied by three is ______________.

C Something Big. Replace the underlined words with the following words.

average ▪ content ▪ mass ▪ one ▪ empty ▪ consists

1 In the middle part of town there was only a single bank.
2 The only things inside of the box were a small teacup and a piece of paper.
3 The food did not taste too good or too bad, it was very normal.
4 Peter's dinner is made up of fruit and water. He doesn't eat much.
5 Ron's paper is clear. He did not write anything on it.
6 The size of Jupiter is much bigger than the Earth.

D Now over to You … Answer the questions using the words from page 136.

1 When baking, what kinds of things do you need to pay attention to?
What about when building a house or making a drink?
2 In section B there are some common facts involving numbers.
Do you know any other common facts that involve numbers? What are they?
3 Do you know how to convert kilogram into pounds?
4 What prime numbers do you know?
5 Can you count backwards from 100?
6 Do you have a lucky number? What is it?

More Numbers!

Quantities

- *At least* four million tourists visit the Grand Canyon every year. Some years there are more tourists.
- John felt that there weren't *enough* hours in the day to finish his work.
- Children *up to* the age of five get in for free. After that they must pay.
- While George's family went on holiday, he had to *remain* behind for his job.
- A *part* of Lisa's coin collection was very expensive. Some of the collection was very cheap.

Dialogues

- The lady who could predict the future said, "Pick a card, *any* card. It does not matter which one."
- Mike asked, "What is that object on the table?" Sarah said, "I don't know what that *thing* is."
- "I'm hungry," said Mark, "does anyone have *something* I can eat?" "I have an apple you can have," said Jenny.

Units of Measure

- The world's longest train had a *length* of 7.3 kilometres.
- A *quarter* of the people said they did not like chocolate. The other 75% said they loved it.
- The distance between the beach and the hotel was one *mile* or about 1.6 kilometres.
- The music was being played at *half* speed. It was twice as slow as normal.
- The earthquake was a 7.0 on the Richter *scale* and caused a lot of damage.
- The metric system is a system of *measure* used all over the world.

A Numbers and Amounts. Unscramble the groups of letters to fill in the blanks in the sentences.

1 There are over six ________________ LBONLII people in the world.

2 The men saw ________________ GSHINTMOE in the sky. They were unsure what it was.

3 In one year there are ________________ EVLWTE months.

4 Many months have only ________________ YTRITH days.

5 A millennium is one ________________ HOTUDSNA years.

6 Nobody was sure what the ________________ GHTNI was for. It was a strange object.

7 The ________________ ECLAS of the map was 1:100.

B Mistakes. Correct the following sentences.

at least ▪ up to ▪ million ▪ fifteen ▪ sixty

1 In tennis the number three represents the first point one gains in a game.
2 There are at most 365 days in a year.
3 There are exactly fifty seconds in a minute.
4 After the age of 18, most people are considered children or teens.
5 There are almost 500 thousand people in the European Union.

C Odd One Out. Circle the word in each group that does not belong.

1 mile – length – measure – remain
2 forty – any – fifty – twenty
3 quarter – part – half – hundred

D Word Scramble. Find eight words from this chapter in the word search.

S	A	Y	X	P	C	V	B	L	N
D	R	E	M	A	I	N	R	E	M
V	Q	S	A	R	G	V	D	N	J
M	W	D	J	T	H	I	N	G	F
E	E	X	V	T	D	J	W	T	S
A	R	N	J	G	S	R	T	H	Z
S	T	R	F	V	C	F	J	J	R
U	Z	E	Q	U	A	R	T	E	R
R	U	I	O	P	L	L	K	J	H
E	I	M	I	L	E	D	D	S	G

E Now over to You … Answer the questions using the words from page 138.

1 How many people live in your house/on your street/in your city/in your country?
2 Describe the rules where you come from. How long is a person a child? When is someone an adult?
3 Describe your monthly budget. How much do you spend on food? How much do you spend on fun?

A Little More

- The city library has a *substantial* amount of books. There are so many they don't have room for them all.
- Many people in the world like to *collect* stamps or coins. Sometimes they have rare stamps in their collections.
- Mark called the hotel for *additional* information. The hotel did not have any more information than he did.
- Jane wants to *increase* her weight, because she thinks she is too thin. Most people want to weigh less, not more.
- Annie wanted a new house, *double* the size of her old one. Her husband wasn't sure what they would do with twice the space.
- The mother taught her daughter how to *count* from 1 to 10. Soon she could count from 1 to 100.

A Trip to the Supermarket

Jenny had to go to the supermarket. Jenny always made a list of the things she needed to buy. The first *item* on her list was milk. Another *component* of her list was fruit. Jenny did not write a specific kind of fruit, because she liked *various* kinds of fruit. At the market, she decided to buy apples. She had to put the apples on a *scale* to find out how much she had, because apples were sold by the kilogram. The last *element* of her list was eggs. After she got the eggs, she decided that she had *enough* food. She had all that she needed. The nice lady at the counter added up her costs and told Jenny her *sum*. The *sum* was 5 Euros. Jenny was happy that she had a good trip to the market.

At the End

- Tim's team lost the football match 1:3. A *loss* does not feel as good as a win.
- Out of a group of eight people, three wanted to go to the cinema. The *rest* wanted to go to a restaurant.
- The *limit* of people that could fit in the car was five. The car was too small for more people.
- The pupil had *sufficient* time for his exam. He was able to finish in the time given him.
- The guitar was *partly* made in the USA. Some of the guitar was also made in China.
- The football team *limits* the number of tickets you can buy. You can only buy two per game.
- The *extent* of Tom's land was marked with a wall. It was at the end of his property.

Odds and Ends

- John needs to *replace* the hand soap in his bathroom. There isn't anything left of the old one.
- A large *proportion* of the children at the school rode the bus in the morning. A small amount of children walked to school.
- Lisa asked Tim if he was sure that the meeting was at 5 pm. Tim said he was *certain* it would be at 5 pm.
- A typical *set* of golf clubs has at least twelve clubs. Many people choose to carry more clubs.

A Definitions. Match the words with their definitions or descriptions.

1	element → b	a	different, diverse
2	replace	b	a part
3	certain	c	to assume the role or position of something else
4	rest	d	a group, collection
5	various	e	exactly what is needed
6	set	f	what is left behind, what remains
7	sufficient	g	sure, to know positively

B Missing Words. Complete the sentences using the following words.

partly ▪ limit ▪ count ▪ scale ▪ sum ▪ component ▪ collect ▪ increase ▪ loss

1 The young lady stood on a ______________ in her bathroom to find out her weight.

2 The teacher told the pupil to ______________ to ten in Spanish.

3 The price of gasoline seems to ______________ every day. It is always more expensive.

4 The city wanted to ______________ the amount of cars on the road. They thought there were too many.

5 Paul likes to ______________ stamps. He has over 500 in his collection.

6 An important ______________ in baking bread is flour. It is probably the most important part.

7 Many older people sometimes have memory ______________. They don't remember as well as they used to.

8 The wall was ______________ destroyed. But most of it was still there.

9 When you add up all the components you get the ______________.

C Synonyms. Replace the underlined words with the following words.

proportion ▪ extent ▪ substantial ▪ enough ▪ item ▪ double ▪ sum ▪ additional

1 The price of coffee was <u>two times</u> that of cola.
2 The <u>total</u> of all the food Mary bought was 30 Euro.
3 There are a <u>large</u> number of trees in the park.
4 One <u>thing</u> on the shopping list was butter.
5 George likes to order his pizza with <u>extra</u> cheese.
6 Jane had <u>the right amount of</u> money to buy a cheeseburger for lunch.
7 The original forest <u>length</u> was very large. Now the forest is much smaller.
8 A small <u>measure</u> of the population is very rich. The largest part is poor.

D Now over to You … Answer the questions using the words from page 140.

1 What is a typical visit to the supermarket like for you?
2 What do you buy? How much do you buy? Do you make a list?
3 Do you or did you collect something when you where younger? What do/did you collect?
Why are/were these objects interesting?

The Same and Different

Goodbye, Grandma!

Paul: Goodbye, Grandma. I am going to meet some friends.
Grandma: *Who* are you going to meet?
Paul: I am going to meet some friends.
Grandma: *What* are you going to do?
Paul: We want to play basketball in the park.
Grandma: In *which* park do you want to play basketball?
Paul: In Central Park! Goodbye!

Sarah's Animals

Sarah has *a* cat, *an* elephant, and *an* alligator. *The* cat's name is Oscar, *the* elephant's is Sam, and *the* alligator's is Susi. She has *a* new horse, too. *This* horse is totally black. Two years ago, Sarah had *a* different horse; *that* horse was white.
Sarah also has many dogs; some are dangerous and some are nice. See *these* dogs? I only touch them when they are close to Sarah. I never touch *those* dogs that are far away from her, alone in the garden. I am afraid of *such* dogs.

The Royal Family

I am very interested in the Royal Family of England. It is my hobby to collect information about them. *I* especially like the Queen because *she* knows how to act and what to do in every situation. *I* do not know much about her husband; *he* is very quiet next to her. Of course *I* know a lot about her children because *they* are in the press and on TV so often. My *own* family and *I* are not as special as the Royal Family; *we* are very normal in comparison. *We* have a normal flat, a normal income and a normal dog. *It* is named Goofy. *I* like the Royal Family so much because *they* live differently. What about *you*? Are *you* interested in a different lifestyle, too?

A What Did You Do Today? Complete the sentences using the following words.

who ▪ where ▪ one ▪ what ▪ an

1 ______________ did you eat for lunch today?

2 ______________ is the last person you like to speak with before going to bed?

3 Name ______________ person with whom you laughed last week.

4 ______________ will you go after finishing these exercises?

5 Do you have ______________ apple in your kitchen right now?

B Girlfriends. Replace the underlined words with the following words.

they ▪ you ▪ she ▪ who ▪ we ▪ we ▪ he

When I was young, my best girlfriend was called Susie, he[1] was a very nice and a pretty girl. She lived with her familiy just around the corner so they[2] could meet as often as we wanted. You[3] had a house which looked almost exactly like ours: it was white with a red front door. Sometimes her brother played with us. It[4] was older than Susie. But more often we played alone in the garden with the cat, we[5] was named Jerry. You[6] were more at Susie's house than with my family. Sometimes my mother even asked: "Why don't they[7] move to your friend's house?"

C Here or There. Unscramble the groups of letters to form the words described in the sentences.

1 MESA ________________: two things that are very similar

2 SMEO ________________: if you have a number of things

3 TANOREH ________________: it is not the same but different

4 SETHO ________________: the things, animals or human beings over there

D At the Video Store. Complete the sentences using the following words.

such ▪ this ▪ that ▪ these ▪ one

Jenny: I want to see a film tonight. The ______________[1] with Al Pacino.

Mark: I do not like ______________[2] American films, I like European films much better.

Jenny: European films? No way! The one with Til Schweiger is ______________[3] a boring film!

Mark: All right, let's not argue, we can find one ______________[4] we both like.

Jenny: Come over here. ______________[5] is the international section. Now let's see ...

E Now over to You ... Answer the questions using the words from page 142.

1 Describe the members of your family. Where do they live? What are their hobbies?
2 If you meet somebody for the first time, what are the first questions you ask?

Inside the Mirror

Before the Trip

Teacher: Good morning, students! There is no math today; we are going to make a trip to the park. Is *everybody* here?

Paul: Seventeen, eighteen, nineteen … No, Miss Smith! *Someone* is missing!

Teacher: Eighteen, nineteen, twenty! No, *everybody* is here, *nobody* is missing.

Sarah: But Paul is right, not everyone has a partner. There is *somebody* missing.

Teacher: Is there *anyone* who does not have a partner?

Paul: Chris does not have *anybody*. His brother is sick today; he is not coming. Let's go to the park!

On Time

Mr. Smith is on time everywhere he goes, *every* day. All his brothers are like Mr. Smith. *Each* of them comes on time. Their sisters, though, are different: *none* of them is ever on time. *Either* they are much too late or they do not come at all. Sometimes the sisters try to be as exact as their brothers but *no one* ever succeeds. This is why family meetings were always a problem until Mr. Smith had an idea: when he invites his brothers and sisters, he gives his brothers the correct time. But he tells his sisters to be there two hours earlier. Most of the time *both* sides come about the same time and are very surprised to meet *each other* on Mr. Smith's front door.

Love Letter

Dear Mary,
I miss you very much! Since you are on holidays there is *nothing* left I like to do. Sometimes I try not to think about you but I cannot concentrate on *whatever* I do instead. I cannot do *anything* until you come back from your trip to the south. I do not know the people with *whom* you spend your time there, but I really hope you enjoy it!
Love, Tim

A People's Positions. Complete the sentences using the following words.

himself ▪ itself ▪ themselves ▪ herself ▪ myself ▪ yourself

1 I always ask _____________ what I should wear on Saturday night.

2 She knows _____________: if she starts eating chocolate she cannot stop until it is finished.

3 The baby is not interested in the other children, it is just interested in _____________.

4 When John sees _____________ in the mirror, he always wants to cut his hair.

5 Do you always wash _____________ after sports?

6 Annie always argues with her parents, they never try to put _____________ in her position.

B Party! Replace the underlined words with the following opposite words.

anyone ▪ everybody ▪ anything ▪ all

Lisa turns 18 years old today. She will have a big party and invite nobody [1] she knows. She hopes that none [2] of them will come. Even people she is not good friends with are invited: no one [3] is welcome! Her family already asked her if she wants something special to eat for this day and Lisa answered, "Just cook nothing [4] you like!"

C Wrong Turn – In the Museum. Replace the underlined words with the following words.

someone ▪ nobody ▪ every ▪ anybody

Mrs. Smith: Look at these books! Each [1] book is beautifully illustrated.
Mr. Smith: Just wonderful! I am sure no one [2] is capable to do such a great work today!
Mrs. Smith: Oh yes, I'm sure there is somebody [3] who still can do this sort of books.
Mr. Smith: What makes you so sure about it?
Mrs. Smith: The sign over there "Contemporary books to sell – anyone [4] interested in antiques, go this way" – we are still in the wrong corner of this museum.

D True or False? Correct the following sentences.

1 Three boys are on their way to school. Both is carrying a big school bag.
2 You have to choose by now: Even she goes or I!
3 If Paul is afraid he puts one arms up to protect his face.
4 I had so many plans for that day! Fortunately I felt free to do nothing I wanted to do!

E Now over to You … Answer the questions using the words from page 144.

1 If you look at old group photos – what could these people have in mind? What could they be thinking?
2 You would like to give a lot of money to a person or an organisation. To whom would you like to give it? Why?
3 With whom do you like to go to the cinema? With whom do you play sports? With whom do you go shopping?

Good Night!

Every night at 11 o'clock Sarah goes to bed, and every morning at 7 o'clock she gets up. Sarah likes to sleep eight hours every night. *From* 11 pm *until* 7 am is exactly the time Sarah needs to not feel tired the next day. Usually she reads a book *by* John Grisham *before* she goes to bed. Sometimes she has dramatic dreams about crime and the police *during* the night. The next morning Sarah does not like to talk to anyone even when she has slept enough. She is not ready to do anything *before* she has had some coffee. Only *after* she has had two cups of coffee, without milk, but with a lot of sugar, does her day start.

Where Are My Keys?

It is always the same old story: I want to leave the house but I can never find my keys. *Since* I cannot find my keys, I will be late once again. My keys are not *on* the table, where they should be. They are not *in* my bag, where they sometimes are. I look *at* my husband outside who is waiting for me in front of the house, but he just shakes his head. He does not have my keys either. I go *into* the kitchen. There I look for them *on* the table, *on* the chairs, and near the window, but my keys have disappeared. *As* I go *to* the front door to leave without them, I suddenly see my keys. They are in the door lock, just waiting for me to leave.

Multi-Tasking – An Interview with George Smith

Telegraph: George, you describe yourself as a multi-tasking young man. Why?

George: I was always a normal student, but since our baby was born last year I do at least three things at the same time: *while* holding the baby, I study and cook dinner.

Telegraph: Are you never tired?

George: Of course I am. Last summer I had a very important examination *whilst* the baby was suffering from a sore throat. This situation was not easy for me, but I knew that I would get *through* it.

Telegraph: If you could choose once again *between* your life *as* a normal student and yours as a multi-tasking father, which one you would pick?

George: The second one! I like to multi-task and *so* I would always pick my life *as* a multi-tasking father!

A Where Is the Cat?

Paul is searching for his little cat. Where does he look?

1 Paul goes __________ the door and looks __________ the kitchen. No cat!

2 He looks under the table and __________ the bag. Still no cat.

3 __________ he does not see the cat under the chair he looks __________ his e-mail messages.

4 Just __________ he leaves the room, he sees the cat under the chair.

B Multi-Tasking George. Write down eight sentences from the chart below. Use each structure word at least once.

George often cooks dinner	since	the baby is asleep.
George usually goes to his math class	whilst	he puts the baby to bed.
He can study for his next exam	during	breakfast and lunch.
He often falls asleep	between	he is holding the baby.
He takes care of the baby	before	a film on TV.
	as	his wife comes home.
	after	he is very tired at night.
	until	he has two hours before his next course.

C J. K. Rowling. Complete the sentences using the following words.

up to ▪ between ▪ by ▪ so ▪ from ▪ as ▪ through ▪ since

Harry Potter is a very popular fantasy-series ______________ [1] the English writer J. K. Rowling. When she wrote her first book, Rowling was ______________ [2] poor as a church mouse, but she made it ______________ [3] these hard times: everything changed ______________ [4] the moment when she published her first volume. ______________ [5] in the beginning no publishing houses wanted to take her story she had to send it to many different ones. Finally one took the manuscript and promised to publish ______________ [6] 500 books. Today every child in England knows the name Harry Potter, and ______________ [7] do children all over the world. One can read Rowling's books in 65 languages now. Today she is considered to be the richest woman in the UK. She has ______________ [8] 1.0 and 1.2 billion US dollars.

D Now over to You … Answer the questions using the words from page 146.

1 What do you do after you get up in the morning? Describe your morning routine using a lot of details.
2 Have you always had the same goals for your future? What are they? Have they changed and how?
3 Do you like to do many things at the same time? What are the advantages and disadvantages of doing a lot of things at once?

House no. 47

The Smith Family lives *inside* house number 47 on Oxford Street. Each member of the family has its own room. The oldest member of the family, grandfather George, lives *on* the first floor *below* his daughter Jenny, who always works on the computer. Jenny's husband Tom usually manages the household. His room is *beside* Jenny's. Tom lives *above* the children's room, who often play cards *inside*. More often, though, the children do not play *inside* but *outside* in the fresh air. *Outside* they either play in the garden *behind* the house or in the street *in front of* the house.

A Letter from Australia

Dear Chris,
I have arrived in Australia. For the first time in my life I have left the UK! It is even the first time I have been *out of* Cornwall! Now I am more than 10,000 miles *away from* home. It took me a very long time to fly all the way *around* the world. I travelled more than 28 hours. I even flew *over* the Himalayas! The farm *where* I work now is about three hours *from* Sydney. For Australians, it is considered *near* the city. *From* the airport I took the bus *to* the farm. We crossed some mountains and the bus went *up* and *down*. Even though I was tired *from* the long journey, I knew that I wanted to stay here from the first moment I stepped *onto* the property.
Love, Linda

Best Friends

Paul and Ron have known each other since their first year of school. In the *past*, they did everything together: they went to the same classes, they had the same hobbies, and they even lived *within* the same apartment building. Of course they also had the same friends, so they were always *among* the same group of people. After college, Paul became a police officer. Ron, however, became involved in crime and illegal activities. From then on, they stopped being friends, and started working *against* each other. Now, when they meet, Paul turns away and Ron does not look *towards* him any longer. Sometimes, Paul even works in an office at the police precinct when Ron is in prison, *beyond* the office on the other side of the wall. It is obvious that they do not move *along* the same path anymore.

Directions

I will give you some directions so you can find my apartment very easily: drive *along* the main road all the way to the end. Then you drive *round* the park and take the first road to the left. From there you will see a bridge. You pass *under* this bridge and move *on to* the next corner. Leave your car in the parking lot on the right-hand side. Then go *across* the street to the house on the other side. You have to climb lots of stairs because my apartment building is *upon* a hill and I live on the sixth floor. I will be waiting for you!

A Animals. Replace the underlined words with the following opposite words.

down ▪ away from ▪ inside ▪ where ▪ under ▪ within ▪ behind

Peter has twelve fish outside[1] his aquarium. There are not only fish but also other living things beyond[2] the aquarium. These living things are red and very beautiful but you can rarely see them because they hide in front of[3] the fish. They always swim near[4] the fish because they are afraid of them. If anything is above them they swim up[5] to the bottom. Like fish, they always have to be over[6] water because they cannot breathe out of the water. Sometimes Peter's parents ask their son, "Where are these things?" But Peter never says there[7] they are. Strangely enough, he is the only one who ever sees them. Perhaps they are not afraid of little boys.

B Sports. Correct the following sentences.

1 Cars usually move across a motorway without stopping. They should only stop when there is a problem.
2 Paul has been a swimmer since he was eight years old. He always loves the moment when he steps below the diving board and jumps into the water.
3 When people play football, one team always plays with the other one. Each team tries to move the ball away from their opponents' goal.
4 Sarah does not like to play football in a professional team. She just likes to play sports without her friends.

C What Happens? Complete the sentences using the following words.

beside ▪ out of ▪ upon ▪ across ▪ below

1 The bank robber broke ______________ jail last night and hasn't been found yet.
2 The football player ran ______________ the field to catch the football.
3 The young woman was sitting ______________ the old man on the train.
4 It is convenient to have a garage ______________ the house.
5 My parent's house is ______________ a hill.

D Word Jumble. Unscramble the groups of letters to form the words described in the sentences.

PUON ______________: a formal word for 'on'

EVABO ______________: if something is directly over another thing or higher than it

NODRU ______________: when there is a corner you move like this

SPTA ______________: further than a particular place

E Now over to You … Answer the questions using the words from page 148.

1 How do you get from your house to your workplace?
2 When you go to see a movie, where do you like to sit? Why?
3 Describe your room. What do you have in your room and where is it?
4 Where are the rooms in your apartment or your house? Do you have a garden or a yard? Where is it?

Paul's and Jenny's Big Day

Paul *and* Jenny are married.

Peter has a big piece *of* cake. Michael's piece *of* cake is even bigger *than* Peter's.

This is a table *without* flowers. That is a table *with* flowers.

Here is a present *for* Annie.

George, get *off* that roof!

Travel Plans

Maria: Paul, do you want to come *to* Hawaii *with* me? Just say "Yes" *or* "No".
Paul: I would like to come *to* Hawaii, but first I have to find out *if* I have enough money.
Maria: The holiday *to* Hawaii will cost 1000 Euro, *including* the flight and the hotel. That is cheap!
Paul: Umm, I do not know *whether* I want to go *to* Hawaii for my next holiday. I am not sure *whether* Hawaii would be interesting. I would like to go *to* Paris.
Maria: Sun and water – that is interesting! How can you say *that* Hawaii isn't interesting?
Paul: Well, I like museums better. Paris has a lot of museums, *such as* the Louvre. Why do you not ask a friend *such as* Lisa to go with you?

Travel Trouble

- Please hurry, *so that* we can take the next bus *to* the airport.
  We slept so late *so that* we do not even have time for coffee.
- Why are you so slow? *Because of* you we will miss our plane!
  I do not want to pay an extra 500 Euros just *because of* you.
- Now we missed the bus *as well as* the plane.
  We can wait for the next plane just *as well as* we can go back to the hotel.
- You made us miss the plane and our holiday! – I still like you, *though*.

Mary's Best Friend

Mary: Timmy, you are my best friend. I have no other friend *like* you. If everybody were *like* you, the world would be a better place.
Timmy: Hmm.
Mary: *Although* you are so nice, some people do not like you. I like you *although* you have bad breath.
Timmy: Hmm.
Mary: What I like *about* you is that you are so quiet, but sometimes I wish I knew more *about* you.
Timmy: Hmm.
Mary: I love you, *but* you are just a dog. It is sad, *but* we cannot change it.
Timmy: Woof!

A Small but Important. Complete the sentences using the following words.

about ▪ if ▪ of ▪ or ▪ than ▪ that

1 Do you want to see a picture ______________ my boyfriend?

2 No, no, I mean ______________ just like I said it.

3 Do you want lasagne ______________ spaghetti for dinner?

4 I will only go to the theatre ______________ you come with me.

5 We talked all night ______________ his plans to go to England.

6 Peter is taller ______________ Paul.

B Mix and Match. Write down eight sentences from the chart below. Use each structure word at least once.

Paul will buy a new car Mike will book a holiday on Maui	although but because as well as so that though including with	he does not know which model. the flight and a nice hotel. he does not have enough money. he has to win the lottery first. his old car broke down. a travel agency in Glasgow. he can get to work faster. he loves his old car.

C Meaningful Words. Unscramble the groups of letters to form the words described in the sentences.

1 I cannot come to your party ________________ ABCEESU my mother will not let me.

2 I do not know ________________ EEHHRTW George will come later or at all.

3 ________________ AGHHLOTU I brought Susie flowers, she did not invite me to her birthday.

4 Lisa hurt my feelings. I miss her, ________________ GHHOTU.

D Now over to You … Answer the questions using the words from page 150.

1 Make at least five comparisons using like and than.
2 Did you ever make a mistake? What happened and why?
3 Complete the following sentences about yourself.

I am learning English because ____.

I am learning English so that ____.

I am learning English although ____.

What I like about learning English is that ____.

I am learning English as well as ____.

Is It Worth It?

Three *plus* five is eight.

The gas costs 1,99 Euro *per* litre.

This bill is *worth* five Euros.

Mary stays inside *due* to the rain.

Lisa and Annie play outside *despite* the rain.

Saturday Night

- This Saturday, *rather than* going to a party again, I would like to stay home.
  I would like to read *rather than* dance tonight.
- Why do you not want to come to the party with me?
  You act *as if* you were 60 years old, *as if* a little bit of music would hurt you.
- Ok, I will come to the party *even though* I do not really feel like it.
- Annie danced *throughout* the whole party.
  Throughout the five hours that the party lasted, she did not sit down even once.
- Annie danced *as though* she would never be able to dance again.
  She danced *as though* the rest of the world did not exist for her.
- The party was a big success, *according to* Annie. *According to* Lisa, it was just too loud.
- Lisa was mad that her mom would not believe her. "Mom, I did not smoke *nor* drink!
  Why do you not believe me *nor* listen to me?"

The Good and Bad Sides of a Job

- I really need the money. I will not do this *unless* I am paid for it. I will leave the company *unless* my boss offers me a better wage.
- *In terms* of money, this job is not good. But *in terms* of social benefits, this job is good.
- *As to* the gain of experience, this is an interesting job. I also cannot complain *as to* the work atmosphere in the company: everybody is really friendly.
- I would rather be in the park *instead* of working in my office all day. I would prefer to have more holidays *instead* of more money.
- My old job paid badly, *whereas* this one pays well. In my old job, I worked 40 hours per week *whereas* in my new job I work at least 50 hours per week.
- A good thing about my job is that *along with* my wage I receive social benefits.

A Car Accident

- Everybody on the street, *apart from* one person, saw the accident.
- I hope the owners have insurance *for* the car.
- *In order to* claim money at an insurance company, you have to fill out a lot of papers.
- Sometimes it is hard to get money from the insurance *even if* you did not cause the accident.
- How much money the insurance pays is *subject to* how much your car is worth.

A How to Live a Happy Life. Complete the sentences using the following words.

as if ▪ despite ▪ even ▪ in order to ▪ rather than ▪ subject to ▪ in terms of

1 ________________ how to live happy, I have some advice.

2 Follow these rules, ________________ live a happy life.

3 To be happy is not ________________ how much money you have.

4 Stay calm, ________________ bad situations.

5 Discuss, ________________ argue.

6 Dance, ________________ no one is watching you.

7 Smile, ________________ when you are sad.

B Happy Peter. Replace the underlined words with the following words.

along with ▪ due to ▪ nor ▪ per ▪ as though ▪ throughout ▪ as to ▪ whereas

1 <u>About</u> Peter's life: he really is much happier now.
2 His 30th birthday came <u>together with</u> an interesting character change.
3 He used to be very quiet, <u>but</u> he is almost wild now.
4 Yesterday Peter acted <u>like</u> he was drunk.
5 He had bought one rose <u>for each</u> girl at the party.
6 Peter talked to girls <u>during</u> the whole evening.
7 <u>Because of</u> his new character he is really popular now.
8 He is not sad <u>and not</u> quiet any more.

C Evaluating. Find the following words in the word search.

according (to) ▪ apart (from) ▪ even (if) ▪ instead (of) ▪ plus ▪ worth

W	O	R	E	V	I	N	G	A
P	L	A	C	C	N	S	A	C
L	R	P	L	U	S	T	U	C
U	W	A	C	C	T	E	N	O
W	O	R	T	H	E	V	E	N
I	O	T	V	M	A	O	R	T
A	C	C	O	R	D	I	N	G
V	A	U	S	S	P	L	A	D

D Now over to You … Answer the questions using the words from page 152.

1 Did you ever do something other people told you not to do? What was it?
2 Do you like your job? Why? What makes it good or bad?
3 When you were a child, what rules did you have to follow? Did you receive money if you helped in the house?

Who Is Peter?

Aiden: Jenny, do you *know* Peter?
Jenny: Yes, I *know* him well.
Aiden: What does he *look* like?
Jenny: He *looks* like he *is* 18, but he *is* 31 years old. Peter *has* blue eyes and red hair. He *comes* from Berlin. He *came* to Frankfurt to visit me for my birthday.
Aiden: Can you *tell* me something else about him?
Jenny: Yes. Peter *is* pretty wild and he *makes* the best cocktails in the world.
Aiden: Oh, now I *think* I *know* him. I *think* I met him at your party last week.

Asking for a Dog

Timmy: Mommy, *can* I please *get* a dog? You *said* when I *turned* twelve I *could get* a cat or a dog.
Mother: But who *will take* the dog outside every day?
Timmy: I *will*! I promise. I *will take* the dog outside every day.
Mother: *Is* that true? Do you really *want* a dog?
Timmy: I always *wanted* a dog. Oh, please *say* yes!
Mother: OK. But you *must take* the dog for a walk every day.
Timmy: Lisa! Mommy *said* yes! Hurray! She really *said* that we *can have* a dog!

Going to the Theatre

Rachel: I want to *go* to the theatre next week. Ron *wants* to *go*, too. Do you *want* to *come* to the theatre with me?
Maria: Yes, I *do*.
Rachel: *Can* you buy tickets tomorrow?
Maria: I *think* I *can*.

Maria: I bought the tickets. Where do you *want* me to *put* them?
Rachel: Just *put* them on the table.

Ron: Did you *see* Annie at the theatre?
Rachel: No, we did not *see* her there.

Too Many Demands

My friend Paul *asks* for things all the time. All day long I hear him *say*:

- Chris, *can* you please *give* me a pen? *Can* you also *give* me a piece of paper?
- Chris, I cannot *find* my keys. *Can* you please *help* me *find* them?
- Chris, *can* I *use* your computer? *Can* I also *use* your biology book tonight?
- Chris, *may* I *have* some of your coffee? *May* I also *take* some of your spaghetti?
- Chris, *can* I *take* your car tonight? I do not *want* to *take* my bike because of the rain.

I really cannot stand it any more.

A At the Door. Complete the sentences using the following words.

can ▪ come ▪ do ▪ has ▪ is ▪ say ▪ will

Jane: Hi, this is Jane. __________ [1] Annie at home?

Mrs. Smith: I am sorry, Annie is not at home.

Jane: Annie still __________ [2] my English book. __________ [3] you know when she comes home?

Mrs. Smith: She said she __________ [4] be back at ten. Would you like to __________ [5] inside and wait for Annie?

Jane: Oh, no, I __________ [6] not wait that long. Thank you. Please __________ [7] hello to her from me.

Mrs. Smith: Of course. Goodbye.

B Mind Maps. What can you give? What can you find? Who/What do you know?
Add as many phrases as you can think of. Also connect phrases to more than one verb if possible.
Make similar mind maps for: see, want, think (of).

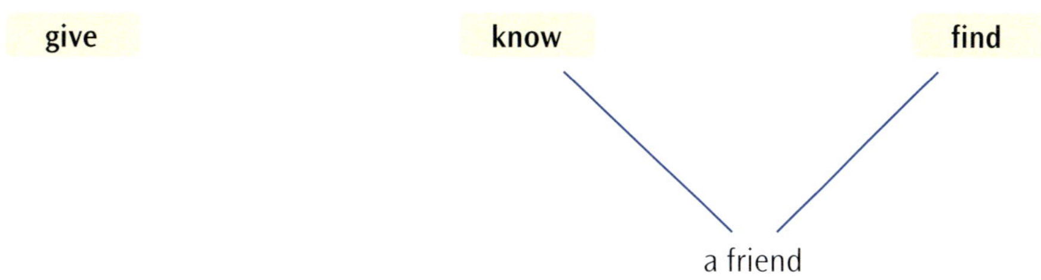

C Child Care. Replace the underlined words with the following words.

go ▪ make ▪ may ▪ must ▪ put ▪ use

1 Are you cold? I will <u>create</u> some tea for you. Do you also want some food?
2 The sun is shining, do you want to <u>sleep</u> outside? You could play in the park with your friends.
3 It is eight o'clock. <u>Must</u> we watch TV now?
4 Dad, Tom wants to <u>share</u> your computer. – Tom, I told you that you may not touch it.
5 You can watch TV, but you <u>want to</u> do the dishes first. – Why is it always me who does the dishes?
6 Thank you for the flowers, Lisa. I will <u>throw</u> them on the table.

D Now over to You … Answer the questions using the words from page 154.

1 Tell someone about a time you heard or saw something funny.
2 When you were a child, was there something you really wanted? What was it? Did you get it?
3 Do you like to share your things? Do you use other people's things? Why or why not?

Going to the Library

- *May* I *ask* you something? Where *is* the library?
- Just *follow* the road and you *will* get there. You *can* also *follow* Mary, she *knows* the way.
- Are you *going* to the library now? *Could* you please *bring* me this book from the library? I *will bring* yours back next time.
- I have to *find* my money. *Can* you please *hold* my books for a second? Thanks for *holding* them.
- If you *have* a problem, *ask* someone who *works* there. They *will help* you.
- Sometimes it *is* difficult to *find* the right book there. If you *need* help, just *ask* someone.

A Long Distance Relationship

- Sarah, you *are* a very nice person. I *like* you very much! *Would* you *like* to *go* out for dinner with me?
- When I *say* "I love you", I *mean* I love you! It does not *mean* anything else.
- Here, *keep* this ring as a sign of my love. Do not ever *give* it away.
- Please, Sarah, do not *leave* me! – I *am* sorry, but I have to *leave* you.
- I *will* miss you, Sarah! Please *call* me whenever you *see* a telephone. – Michael, I *will call* you as soon as I get to London.

Doctors and Patients

- When Tim was a child and someone *asked* him, "Timmy, what do you want to *become* when you *are* an adult?", he answered, "I *want* to *become* a doctor." Now Tim *is* done with school, and *will begin* to *go* to university. He *wants* to *begin* his studies in the fall. His parents cannot *provide* enough money for the programme. But the university *provides* a grant for Tim. He *will* also *work* to earn some money. As a student, he *can work* in a restaurant or bar.
- Yesterday I did not *feel* well. I went to the doctor and he gave me some medicine. Today I *feel* much better. At first it *seemed* to *be* a heart problem. Now the doctor *says* that I *felt* bad due to low blood pressure. The doctor said that my weight *seems* too high to him. He said I have to *start* to exercise. I decided that I will *start* tomorrow. The doctor said I *should run* five miles every day. I *think* I would like to *run* in the forest.

A New Haircut

Jenny: Linda, do you *know* how to cut hair?
Linda: No, but I *can try*.
Jenny: Oh no, I do not *want* you to *try* with my hair.
Linda: Oh, do not worry, Jenny. I am *going to* try to *make* it *look* nice. I am not *going to* cut your hair so it *looks* bad. I also cut Lisa's hair and it *looks* really pretty. People *turn* their heads when she walks by. Hey Lisa, *can* you *come* here for a second? I *want* you to *show* your haircut to Jenny.
Jenny: Ok, I *might* give it a try. Afterwards I *might* be mad, though.

A Mind Maps. Use the following words to make mind maps.

to begin ▪ to bring ▪ to need ▪ to start ▪ to become

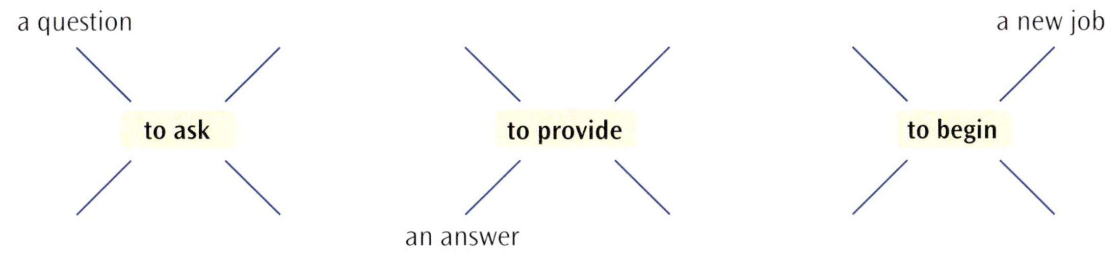

B Not Quite True. Replace the underlined words with the following opposite words.

am going to ▪ held ▪ keep ▪ like ▪ seems ▪ turn

1 It is certain that he does not have a lot of money.
2 Mom said you should release the bird.
3 I dropped the ball.
4 Go straight left after the bank.
5 I hate flowers.
6 I will not give them water.

C Nice Weather. Complete the sentences using the following words.

work ▪ tried ▪ call ▪ mean ▪ feels ▪ asked ▪ think ▪ become

1 After four weeks of rain the sun is shining today. It ______________ very nice.
2 It would be nice to go to the lake. Too bad I have to ______________ today.
3 May I use your phone? I will ______________ the office and ask for the day off.
4 Too bad I could not get the day off. Oh well, at least I ______________.
5 What do you ______________ when you say I do not like to work?
6 This weekend the weather will ______________ even warmer. We can go to the lake then.
7 My sister ______________ me if I could pick her up tomorrow.
8 I ______________ helping people is a good thing.

D Now over to You … Answer the questions using the words from page 156.

1 What do you want to become one day? What do you need to do to reach that goal?
2 Did you ever make plans to start something new? What did you do? Did it work?
3 In your culture, what do you do when you like someone? Do you buy flowers for her/him? Do you hold his/her hand?

1.01

A *right*: 1, 3, 4 – *wrong*: 2
B kid – youth – adult – senior
C 1 name – 2 age – 3 name – 4 identify – 5 person – 6 sex – 7 born

1.02 ▪ 1.03

A 1 mother – 2 husband – 3 son – 4 daughter – 5 brother, sister – 6 adopted – 7 parents
B 1e – 2b – 3a – 4c – 5d
C 1 relationship – 2 child – 3 generation – 4 mum – 5 birth – 6 dad
D 1 foreign – 2 French – 3 Europe

1.04 ▪ 1.05

A 1 beautiful – 2 huge – 3 small – 4 tiny – 5 bright – 6 famous
B 1 fair – 2 firm – 3 attracted – 4 unable – 5 appears – 6 skills
C 1 old – 2 confidence – 3 nice – 4 tall

1.06

A *across:* truth, belief, duty, spirit, shall
down: faith, religion, church
diagonal: mass
B 1 religion – 2 Jesus – 3 spirit – 4 help – 5 mass – 6 gods – 7 believe – 8 commitment – 9 truth – 10 exist – 11 shall
C 1 faith – 2 responsible – 3 truth – 4 existing – 5 believe – 6 existence

2.01 ▪ 2.02 I

A 1 floor – 2 house – 3 to let – 4 domestic
B 1 address – 2 estate – 3 block – 4 castle – 5 flat – 6 kitchen – 7 station – 8 castle – 9 garden
C *across:* build, wall
down: room, house, pets, gate

2.02 II ▪ 2.03

A 1 board, yard – 2 key, package, tape – 3 bed, cabinet, table
B 1 entry – 2 hall – 3 shelf – 4 sheet – 5 cover – 6 seat – 7 desk – 8 household – 9 objects
C *across:* package, sheet, bedroom, desk
down: tape, hall
diagonal: seat, object

3.01

A *country:* Africa, France, Germany
county: Cornwall, Devon, Kent
city: London, Paris, Berlin
town: Canterbury, York, Chelmsford
village: individual solutions
B 1 regions – 2 District – 3 countries – 4 park – 5 counties – 6 islands – 7 capital – 8 border
C 1 United States of America – 2 Africa – 3 Europe – 4 Japan – 5 Australia

3.02 I

A 1h – 2i – 3a – 4g – 5b – 6c – 7f – 8e – 9d
B 1 lake, pool, sea – 2 rock, stone, mountain – 3 air, sky, atmosphere
C *across:* 1 environment – 6 hole – 8 natural – 9 forest – 11 water – 13 rural – 15 hill – 16 wave
down: 2 resource – 3 earth – 4 temperature – 5 rain – 7 star – 9 field – 10 river – 11 world – 12 wind – 14 lake

3.02 II ▪ 3.03

A 1 true – 2 false *(Animals that live at your house are considered domesticated.)* – 3 false *(A fish is a type of animal.)* – 4 true – 5 false *(A valley separates mountains.)*
B 1 valley – 2 growth – 3 coast
C 1 dog – 2 horse – 3 cat – 4 human – 5 bird – 6 fish – 7 animals

4.01 I

A 1 north – 2 west – 3 south – 4 east
B 1 forward – 2 out – 3 away – 4 down – 5 up – 6 over
C 1 drive – 2 return – 3 far – 4 arrive

4.01 II

A 1 sign – 2 post – 3 library – 4 map – 5 track
B 1 direction – 2 straight – 3 somewhere – 4 direct
C 1 access – 2 right – 3 near – 4 through – 5 along

4.02 ▪ 4.03

A *across:* 1 travels – 2 drive – 3 train – 4 engine – 5 passage – 6 ship – 7 journey – 8 aircraft – 9 street
down: transport
B 1 path – 2 boat – 3 driver
C 1 drive, lane – 2 stop, cross – 3 route – 4 driver, vehicle

5.01

A 1 their – 2 her – 3 his – 4 my – 5 our – 6 your – 7 Its
B 1 owner – 2 loan – 3 spend – 4 pay – 5 payment – 6 due
C 1 consumer – 2 personal – 3 own – 4 expenditures – 5 sale – 6 whose – 7 acquired

5.02 ▪ 5.03 I

A 1 money, price – 2 expensive, afford – 3 rich – 4 cheap – 5 cost – 6 credit, cash – 7 open
B 1 value – 2 bank – 3 pound – 4 produces – 5 product – 6 business – 7 trade – 8 fee

5.03 II ▪ 5.04

A *across:* enterprise, deliver
down: pocket, ring, wear, manage
B 1 corporation – 2 managing – 3 wear – 4 distribution – 5 deliver – 6 customers
C 1d – 2e – 3a – 4c – 5b
D 1 fashions – 2 dresses – 3 look – 4 exchange

6.01

A 1 lip – 2 mouth – 3 heart – 4 eye – 5 tooth – 6 shoulder – 7 hair – 8 ear – 9 finger – 10 blood
C 1 physical – 2 voice – 3 sleep – 4 joint – 5 brain – 6 back – 7 skin

6.02 I ▪ 6.03

A 1 accident – 2 bloody – 3 injury – 4 doctor – 5 appointment – 6 operation – 7 pain – 8 rest
B 1 death – 2 injury – 3 to hurt – 4 dad
C 1 disease – 2 suffering – 3 breath – 4 vital – 5 die – 6 medical – 7 drugs – 8 survive

6.02 II ▪ 6.04 ▪ 6.05

A 1 food – 2 life – 3 live – 4 health – 5 clean – 6 restaurants – 7 cut
C 1 acid – 2 tea – 3 wine – 4 coffee – 5 drink
D *verbs:* eat, drink, feed
nouns: meal, food, drink
meals: dinner, lunch

7.01

A 1 to push – 2 to carry – 3 to pull – 4 to stick – 5 to shake – 6 to blow – 7 to pick
B 1 walks – 2 stand – 3 sits – 4 leans – 5 covers – 6 removes – 7 hands
C 1 staring – 2 lie – 3 slips – 4 Climbing – 5 clear

7.02

A 1 noise – 2 warm – 3 cold – 4 dark – 5 hear – 6 sharp – 7 hot
B 1 silence – 2 dry – 3 balance – 4 quiet – 5 hard
C *eye:* see, sight ....
ear: listen, hear, sound, noise ...
hand: touch, feel ...
D 1 touch – 2 bright – 3 nervous – 4 angry – 5 loud – 6 old – 7 soft, hard – 8 warm

7.03 I

A 1 drop – 2 silence – 3 sit
B *across:* 1 motion – 2 flows – 3 move – 4 enter – 5 jumped – 6 send – 7 transfer – 8 throw
down: movement
C 1 rise – 2 quick – 3 fell – 4 transfer
D *to ride:* the underground, a train, a bus ....
to fall down: a child, a cup, an apple ...
to fly: a paper airplane, a bird ...
to rise: a balloon, the sun ...

7.03 II ▪ 7.04 ▪ 7.05 I

A *positive:* to smile, to laugh, pleasure, surprise, happy
negative: to worry, sad, shot, fall, tears, fear, afraid

B 1 fast – 2 shots – 3 reason – 4 view – 5 rolled – 6 surprise – 7 remember – 8 pleasure – 9 mind

C 2 *When someone* is afraid... – 3 ...*when they are* happy – 5 *Most parents* worry ...

7.05 II

A 1 notice – 2 influence – 3 mind – 4 reaction

B 1 forgets – 2 serious – 3 reality

C 1 discovered – 2 reasonable – 3 wonder

D 1 experience – 2 realises – 3 ignore

E 1c – 2d – 3b – 4a

7.05 III ▪ 7.06

A 1 to impose – 2 to receive – 3 desire – 4 to wish – 5 need

B 1 mental – 2 satisfied – 3 necessary – 4 recognition – 5 estimates – 6 recall – 7 force – 8 intended

C *across:* maintain, concern, require, demand, select, expect
down: retain, cope, need, dream

8.01 ▪ 8.02 I

A 1 to apply – 2 plan – 3 executive meeting – 4 captain – 5 secretary

B 1 worker – 2 executive, manager – 3 guide – 4 agent

C 1 task – 2 employer – 3 expert – 4 chief – 5 director – 6 farmer – 7 colleague – 8 officer – 9 design – 10 executive

8.02 II

A 1 arrangement – 2 appointed – 3 release – 4 working – 5 conduct – 6 organised

B 1 panel – 2 file – 3 tool – 4 busy – 5 checks

C 1 operate – 2 reference – 3 order – 4 prepare – 5 marketing – 6 release – 7 professional – 8 arranged

8.03

A 1 firm – 2 office – 3 factory – 4 department – 5 farm

B 1d – 2g – 3f – 4h – 5c – 6b – 7e – 8i – 9a

C 1 works – 2 revenue – 3 employ – 4 labour – 5 employment – 6 career – 7 engineering – 8 mechanisms – 9 function

8.04 I

A *down:* 1 competition – 2 strong – 3 level
across: 4 target – 5 power – 6 opposition

B 1 ready – 2 better – 3 success – 4 chance – 5 benefit – 6 attempted

C 1 to lose – 2 failure – 3 opposition – 4 power

8.04 II ▪ 8.05 I

A 1 to run – 2 medium – 3 objective – 4 powerful

B 1f – 2d – 3a – 4b – 5c – 6e

C source, basis, principle – theory, base, model – to examine, to research, to develop

D *across:* winner, theory, effect
down: solution, victory, result, concept

8.05 II ▪ 8.06 I

A *across:* module, scientific, learn, university
down: studies, difficult, generate
diagonal: observe

B 1 observations – 2 staff – 3 student – 4 classes – 5 failed

C 1 course – 2 scientist – 3 experiment – 4 subjects – 5 pass – 6 school – 7 education

8.06 II

A 1 students – 2 discipline – 3 master's degree – 4 concentration – 5 teaching – 6 professor

B educational – 2 assessment – 3 exercise – 4 examination – 5 presence – 6 learning

C 1b – 2g – 3a – 4c – 5f – 6e – 7d

9.01 ▪ 9.02 I

A 1 information – 2 of course – 3 proposed – 4 speech – 5 expressed – 6 sentence

B 1 language – 2 expression – 3 speaker – 4 question

C 1 announced – 2 talking – 3 proposal – 4 why – 5 meaning – 6 detailed

D 1c – 2d – 3a – 4b

9.02 II

B 1 talk – 2 answer – 3 please – 4 explanation – 5 thanks – 6 sorry – 7 example – 8 for example
C 1e – 2d – 3b – 4c – 5a

9.02 III ▪ 9.03 I

A 1 so – 2 mention – 3 i.e. – 4 statement – 5 determined – 6 indicated – 7 stated
B 1 repeat – 2 lies – 3 description – 4 conclusion – 5 describe – 6 noted – 7 there are – 8 refers – 9 points
C 1f – 2d – 3c – 4e – 5a – 6b

9.03 II ▪ 9.04 I

A 1 advised – 2 emphasized – 3 informed – 4 reminded – 5 claimed – 6 implied – 7 However – 8 shouted – 9 concluded
B 1b – 2e – 3a – 4c – 5d – 6g – 7f
C 1 Therefore – 2 decides – 3 discussing – 4 considers – 5 indeed – 6 rather – 7 Thus

9.04 II

A 1 insisted on discussing – 2 doubt – 3 intention
B 1 impression – 2 to persuade – 3 aspect
C 1 Nevertheless – 2 voice – 3 anyway – 4 though – 5 instead – 6 otherwise
D *across:* aspect, idea, debate
down: opinion, approach, decision, doubt, fact

10.01 ▪ 10.02 I

A art, artist, theatre, film – to write, writer, author, to read – to sing, band, music, to perform
B 1 report – 2 scene – 3 gallery
C 1 cultural – 2 books – 3 role – 4 photographs – 5 displayed – 6 song – 7 concert – 8 culture

10.02 II

A 1 sometimes – 2 once a day – 3 asking questions – 4 to write your name – 5 weekly
B *article:* to publish, to illustrate, page, review …
to illustrate: chapter, page, publication, book …
press: to publish, report, to note …
C 1 reading – 2 theme – 3 introduction – 4 document – 5 message
D 1 literature – 2 reader – 3 list – 4 writing – 5 papers

10.03 ▪ 10.04

A 1 player – 2 holiday – 3 effort – 4 interest – 5 league
B 1 picture – 2 used – 3 holidays – 4 play – 5 to aim – 6 struck – 7 championship – 8 interested
C 1d – 2c – 3e – 4a – 5b
D 1 pub – 2 trip – 3 interest

11.01

A to attach, to rely on, to depend on – contact, connection, to introduce, communication – concern, to avoid
B 1 concern – 2 to avoid – 3 present
C 1 row – 2 attached – 3 present – 4 share – 5 promised – 6 accept – 7 influenced – 8 affect

11.02 ▪ 11.03 I

A 1 want – 2 live – 3 tell – 4 tries to be – 5 goes out
B 1 marry – 2 alone – 3 sexual – 4 partner – 5 marriage – 6 trust – 7 pair – 8 love
C 1g – 2f – 3a – 4h – 5b – 6d – 7c – 8e
D couple – group – committee – party

11.03 II

A 1 guest – 2 responsibility – 3 crowd – 4 individual – 5 leadership
B 1 visitor – 2 contribution – 3 civil
C 1 visited – 2 poor – 3 everyone – 4 bar – 5 membership – 6 led – 7 associated – 8 contributed

12.01 ▪ 12.02 I

A to attend, to emerge, to handle, to happen – affair, incident, occasion, situation – government, minister, president, union
B 1f – 2a – 3g – 4b – 5h – 6c – 7d – 8e
C 1 background – 2 political – 3 campaign – 4 attention – 5 national – 6 important – 7 current – 8 issue – 9 matter

12.02 II

A 1 reform – 2 election – 3 equal – 4 conservative – 5 vote – 6 elected – 7 initiative – 8 assembly 9 – international

B 1 lord – 2 ministry – 3 politics

C 1c – 2f – 3h – 4e – 5g – 6b – 7d – 8a

12.03 ▪ 12.04

A 1 shoot – 2 threat – 3 strategy – 4 force – 5 representative – 6 regulations – 7 liberal – 8 gun – 9 leading

B 1 United – 2 weapon – 3 army – 4 defence – 5 majority - 6 Revolution – 7 independent – 8 candidates

C 1 peace – 2 strike – 3 treaty

13.01

A 1 output – 2 market – 3 finance – 4 oil – 5 development – 6 economic – 7 investment – 8 gold – 9 shares

B 1 gas – 2 farm – 3 rate

C 1d – 2h – 3i – 4 g – 5c – 6a – 7e – 8b – 9f

13.02 ▪ 13.06 I

A 1e – 2f – 3i – 4c – 5d – 6g – 7b – 8a – 9h

B 1 code – 2 police – 3 claim – 4 catch – 5 appeal – 6 prove – 7 charge – 8 prison – 9 judge

C 1 bill – 2 contract – 3 crime

13.03

A 1 public – 2 insurance – 3 housing – 4 agency – 5 pension – 6 official – 7 authority – 8 enable – 9 policy

B 1 elderly – 2 social – 3 support

C 1 aid – 2 offer – 3 local – 4 service – 5 serve – 6 public

13.04

A 1c – 2a – 3e – 4h – 5g – 6f – 7b – 8d

B 1 complete – 2 form – 3 traditional – 4 society – 5 process – 6 progress – 7 choice – 8 control – 9 option

C 1 establish – 2 head – 3 purpose – 4 represent – 5 procedure – 6 control – 7 act – 8 provision

13.05

A 1 user – 2 record – 3 radio

B 1g – 2b – 3h – 4c – 5a – 6d – 7e – 8f

C 1 technique – 2 studio – 3 machine – 4 technical

D *across:* record, programme, computer, phone, machine, telephone
down: user, network, radio, call, device, software

13.06 II ▪ 13.07

A 1 danger – 2 fire – 3 enquiry – 4 investigation – 5 careful – 6 security – 7 attack

B 1c – 2e – 3f – 4d – 5a – 6g – 7b

C 1 attack – 2 ensure – 3 investigate – 4 victim – 5 protection – 6 warn – 7 secure

14.01

A 1 space – 2 cell – 3 broad – 4 extended – 5 inside – 6 central – 7 set – 8 placing – 9 area

B 1 under – 2 sector – 3 site – 4 deep – 5 bottom – 6 around – 7 below – 8 front – 9 surface

C 1 central – 2 front – 3 internal

14.02 ▪ 14.03 I

A 1 shape – 2 as fast as lightning – 3 The price of the car included … – 4 My mother really liked it, too. – 5 Both – 6 kind

B 1e – 2c – 3a – 4d – 5b

C 1 together – 2 different – 3 figure – 4 colours – 5 patterns – 6 other – 7 round – 8 not – 9 points

14.03 II

A 1 varies – 2 combined – 3 else – 4 either – 5 type – 6 Relative – 7 variety

B 1 combination – 2 to compare – 3 elsewhere

C *across:* 1 division – 5 distinction – 9 variety
down: 2 variation – 3 advantage – 4 difference – 6 similar – 7 common – 8 copy

D like – common – variation – difference – distinction

14.04 I

A first, second, third, fourth – series, to continue, regular – last, latter, previous
B 1 opening – 2 often – 3 usual – 4 next – 5 end
C 1e – 2d – 3g – 4b – 5a – 6f
D *across:* end, implication, cause
down: following, also, link

14.04 II ▪ 14.09 I

A 1f – 2h – 3g – 4i – 5b – 6a – 7e – 8c – 9d
B 1 impossible – 2 frequent – 3 off – 4 appropriate – 5 sure – 6 on – 7 at all – 8 rare
C 1 row – 2 selection – 3 rare – 4 formal

14.05 ▪ 14.06 ▪ 14.07 I

A 1 middle – 2 priority – 3 effective – 4 easy – 5 interesting – 6 right – 7 ultimate – 8 exact
B 1 bad – 2 difficult – 3 slight – 4 wrong
C *true:* 3, 4, 7, 8
false: 1, 2, 5, 6

14.07 II ▪ 14.09 II

A 1 alright – 2 severe – 3 stages – 4 constant – 5 typical – 6 major – 7 critical – 8 degree – 9 key
B 1 relevant – 2 pretty – 3 overall – 4 importance – 5 basic – 6 criterion – 7 essential – 8 primary – 9 main
C 1b – 2d – 3a – 4f – 5c – 6e

14.08

A 1i – 2e – 3f – 4g – 5c – 6b – 7a – 8h – 9d
B *across:* narrow, normal, familiar, particular
down: specific, modern, light, complex
C 1 rough – 2 thick – 3 real – 4 original – 5 precise – 6 ordinary – 7 wide – 8 clear – 9 special

15.01 I

A 1 Today – 2 always – 3 early – 4 no longer – 5 late – eventually – 7 never – 8 still
B 1 circumstance – 2 now – 3 later – 4 then – 5 When – 6 present – 7 yet
C final, finish – initial, to start – moment, while

15.01 II ▪ 15.02 I

A 1 evening – 2 night – 3 morning – 4 present – 5 brief – 6 day
B 1 term – 2 period – 3 prospects – 4 last – 5 phase – 6 immediate – 7 time – 8 months
C 1c – 2e – 3d – 4a – 5b – 6f

15.02 II

B 1e – 2f – 3g – 4a – 5c – 6b – 7d
C 1 tonight – 2 tomorrow – 3 afternoon – 4 Saturday – 5 Sunday – 6 Friday

15.03

A 1 former – 2 back – 3 earlier – 4 possible – 5 recent – 6 future – 7 unlikely
B 1 future – 2 certainly – 3 soon
C 1 already – 2 Once – 3 Maybe – 4 past – 5 potential – 6 derive – 7 history
D *across:* ago, ancient, past, back, future
down: soon, recent, history

16.01 I

A 1 reduce – 2 more than – 3 lot – 4 much – 5 a bit – 6 more – 7 less – 8 almost
B single – few – many – most – all
C bit, little, only – much, more, the most – everything, total, whole

16.01 II ▪ 16.02 I

A 1e – 2f – 3a – 4c – 5i – 6g – 7b – 8d – 9h
B 1 large – 2 long – 3 entire – 4 full – 5 increasing – 6 less – 7 Several – 8 a little – 9 many
C 1 increase – 2 considerable – 3 big – 4 section – 5 number – 6 total – 7 mere – 8 piece – 9 single

16.02 II ▪ 16.03 I

A 1 size – 2 three – 3 eight
B 1 Half – 2 five – 3 seven – 4 four – 5 percent – 6 six – 7 fit – 8 two – 9 nine
C 1 one – 2 content – 3 average – 4 consists – 5 empty – 6 mass

16.03 II ▪ 16.04 I

A 1 billion – 2 something – 3 twelve – 4 thirty – 5 thousand – 6 thing – 7 scale

B 1 fifteen – 2 at least – 3 sixty – 4 Up to – 5 million

C 1 remain – 2 any – 3 hundred

D *across:* remain, thing, quarter, mile
down: measure, part, scale, length

16.04 II

A 1b – 2c – 3g – 4f – 5a – 6d – 7e

B 1 scale – 2 count – 3 increase – 4 limit – 5 collect – 6 component – 7 loss – 8 partly – 9 sum

C 1 double – 2 sum – 3 substantial – 4 item – 5 additional – 6 enough – 7 extent – 8 proportion

17.01 I

A 1 What – 2 Who – 3 one – 4 Where – 5 an

B 1 she – 2 we – 3 they – 4 He – 5 who – 6 we – 7 you

C 1 same – 2 some – 3 another – 4 those

D 1 one – 2 these – 3 such – 4 that – 5 This

17.01 II

A 1 myself – 2 herself – 3 itself – 4 himself – 5 yourself – 6 themselves

B 1 everybody – 2 all – 3 anyone – 4 anything

C Every – 2 nobody – 3 someone – 4 anybody

D 1 Each – 2 Either – 3 both – 4 anything

17.02 ▪ 17.03 I

A 1 to, into – 2 in(to) – 3 Since, at – 4 before

C 1 by – 2 as – 3 through – 4 from – 5 Since – 6 up to – 7 so – 8 between

17.03 II

A 1 inside – 2 within – 3 behind – 4 away from – 5 down – 6 under – 7 where

B 1 along – 2 onto – 3 against – 4 with

C 1 out of – 2 across – 3 beside – 4 below – 5 upon

D upon – above – round – past

17.04 I

A 1 of – 2 that – 3 or – 4 if – 5 about – 6 than

C 1 because – 2 whether – 3 Although – 4 though

17.04 II

A 1 In terms of – 2 in order to – 3 subject to – 4 despite – 5 rather than – 6 as if – 7 even

B 1 As to – 2 along with – 3 whereas – 4 as though – 5 per – 6 throughout – 7 Due to – 8 nor

C *across:* plus, worth, even, according
down: apaprt, instead

18.01 I

A 1 Is – 2 has – 3 Do – 4 will – 5 come – 6 can – 7 say

C 1 make – 2 go – 3 May – 4 use – 5 must – 6 put

18.01 II

B 1 seems – 2 keep – 3 held – 4 Turn – 5 like – 6 am going to

C 1 feels – 2 work – 3 call – 4 tried – 5 mean – 6 become – 7 asked – 8 think

Arbeitsanweisungen

ENGLISCH	DEUTSCH
Add the following words to the body parts.	Ordnen Sie die folgenden Wörter den Körperteilen zu.
Can you find more words to add to the mindmaps?	Finden Sie weitere Wörter um das Wörternetz zu ergänzen?
Answer the questions using the words from page (xxx).	Beantworten Sie die Fragen. Benutzen Sie dafür die Wörter von Seite (…).
Arrange them into two lists.	Ordnen Sie sie in zwei Spalten ein.
Assign a job to each of the following images.	Ordnen Sie jedem Bild einen Beruf zu.
Assign each of the following words to the picture or fill in the blanks.	Ordnen Sie die folgenden Wörter dem Bild zu oder ergänzen Sie den Text.
Choose one of the underlined words to complete the sentences.	Wählen Sie eins der unterstrichenen Wörter, um die Sätze zu ergänzen.
Circle the word in each group that does not belong.	Kreisen Sie in jeder Gruppe das Wort ein, das nicht dazu passt.
Complete the crossword puzzle using the clues provided.	Füllen Sie das Kreuzworträtsel mithilfe der Hinweise aus.
Complete the crossword puzzle with the following words.	Füllen Sie das Kreuzworträtsel mit den folgenden Wörtern aus.
Complete the sentences using the following words.	Ergänzen Sie die Sätze mit den folgenden Wörtern.
Complete these sentences about yourself. Compare with someone else if possible.	Ergänzen Sie die Sätze über Ihre Person. Wenn es möglich ist, vergleichen Sie mit einer anderen Person.
Correct the following sentences.	Korrigieren Sie die folgenden Sätze.
Determine whether each sentence is true or false. For false sentences, provide a correct alternative.	Bestimmen Sie, ob die folgenden Sätze richtig oder falsch sind. Korrigieren Sie die falschen Sätze.
Draw a stickfigure and label the following body parts.	Zeichnen Sie ein Strichmännchen und beschriften Sie die Körperteile.
Draw images and label them using the following words.	Zeichnen Sie kleine Bilder und beschriften Sie sie mit den folgenden Wörtern.
Fill the gaps with a preposition.	Ergänzen Sie den Text mit den passenden Präpositionen.
Find (...) words from this chapter in the word search.	Finden Sie (…) Wörter dieses Kapitels im Wörtergitter.
Find the following words in the word search.	Finden Sie die folgenden Wörter im Wörtergitter.
How many words from page (xxx) can you find in the puzzle?	Wieviele Wörter von Seite (…) können Sie im Wörtergitter finden?
Label the countries and continents.	Beschriften Sie die Länder und Kontinente.
Label the pictures with the following words.	Beschriften Sie die Bilder mit den folgenden Wörtern.

ENGLISCH	DEUTSCH
Look at a map and fill the gaps with the correct direction.	Ergänzen Sie die passende Himmelsrichtung mithilfe einer Karte.
Match the following words with the pictures.	Ordnen Sie die Wörter den passenden Bildern zu.
Match the words with their definitions or descriptions.	Ordnen Sie den Wörtern die passende Definition oder Erklärung zu.
Organise the following words into categories according to their meaning and add other words and expressions you know.	Ordnen Sie die folgenden Wörter nach ihrer Bedeutung und ergänzen Sie weitere Wörter und Ausdrücke.
Organise the following words into the three categories below.	Ordnen Sie die folgenden Wörter den drei Kategorien zu.
Organise the following words into three categories based on their common meaning.	Ordnen Sie die folgenden Wörter nach ihrer Bedeutung in drei Kategorien ein.
Organise the words into pairs.	Ordnen Sie die Wörter nach Paaren.
Put the following words in order.	Bringen Sie die folgenden Wörter in die richtige Reihenfolge.
Replace the underlined phrases with a word from page (xxx).	Ersetzen Sie die unterstrichenen Ausdrücke mit einem Wort von Seite (...).
Replace the underlined words with the following words.	Ersetzen Sie die unterstrichenen Wörter durch folgende Wörter.
Replace the underlined words with the following opposite words.	Ersetzen Sie die unterstrichenen Wörter durch das Gegenteil.
Replace the underlined words with the following similar words.	Ersetzen Sie die unterstrichenen Wörter durch ähnliche Wörter.
Rewrite the underlined phrases using one of the following words. Sometimes you need to change the sentence structure or the word order.	Formulieren Sie die unterstrichenen Audrücke um. Benutzen Sie dafür die folgenden Wörter. Manchmal müssen Sie die Satzstruktur oder die Reihenfolge der Wörter ändern.
Rewrite them to make them true, from your point of view.	Formulieren Sie die Sätze um. Was ist Ihrer Meinung nach wahr?
Tick the right box.	Kreuzen Sie das passende Kästchen an.
Unscramble the groups of letters to fill in the blanks in the sentences.	Entwirren Sie die Buchstabengruppen und ergänzen Sie die Sätze mit den passenden Wörtern.
Unscramble the groups of letters to form the words described in the sentences.	Entwirren Sie die Buchstabengruppen und formen Sie die Wörter, die in den Sätzen beschrieben sind.
Use the following words and add more words you know.	Benutzen Sie die folgenden Wörter und ergänzen Sie weitere Wörter, die Sie kennen.

ENGLISCH	DEUTSCH
Use the following words to make mind maps.	Benutzen Sie die folgenden Wörter um Wortnetze zu bilden.
Use words from page (xxx) and add more words you know.	Benutzen Sie die Wörter von Seite (...) und ergänzen Sie weitere Wörter, die Sie kennen.
Using page (xxx) and a map of Britain find examples for the following categories.	Benutzen Sie Seite (...) und eine Karte von Großbritannien, um Beispiele für die folgenden Kategorien zu finden.
Which colours do you associate with these nouns?	Welche Farben verbinden Sie mit den folgenden Substantiven?
Write down eight sentences from the chart below. Use each structure word at least once.	Bilden Sie aus der Tabelle acht Sätze. Benutzen Sie jedes Strukturwort mindestens einmal.